OVER CHINA

The publishers thank the following
for their support, without which this book
would not have been possible:

Bond Corporation Holdings Limited

Cathay Pacific Airways Limited

DHL International

Hill and Knowlton

Hutchison Whampoa Limited

ICI (China) Limited

Shell Companies in Hong Kong and China

Sheraton Asia-Pacific Corporation

OVER CHINA

Photography by
Dan Budnik, Georg Gerster, Paul Lau,
Wu Shouzhuang and Jerry Young

Text by Kevin Sinclair
Foreword by Harrison Salisbury

INTERCONTINENTAL
PUBLISHING CORPORATION

Publishers
KEVIN WELDON
JOHN OWEN

Project Director
ROBERT CAVE-ROGERS

Special Consultants
DR STEPHEN FITZGERALD
PETER FORSYTHE

Text Consultant
RENATA ATKINS

Managing Editor
BEVERLEY BARNES

Editor
SHEENA COUPE

Editorial Assistants
ANNE GREENSALL
TRACEY PEAKMAN

Designer
JOHN BULL,
THE BOOK DESIGN CO.

Map
STAN LAMOND,
THE BOOK DESIGN CO.

Picture Editors
PATRICIA DAVIS
NOELINE KELLY
JANE SYMONS

Location Consultant
PAUL LAU

Production Manager
MICK BAGNATO

Balloon Pilots
MIKE BRADLEY
DAWN BRADLEY
DOUG GAGE
PAUL GIANNIOTIS
GARRY OGG
RON PATTINSON
ADAM TAKASH

Balloon Coordinator
SALLY RODWELL

CHINA GREAT WALL PUBLISHING HOUSE

and

CHINA NATIONAL PUBLISHING
INDUSTRY TRADING CORPORATION

Publishers
LIN TINGSONG
ZHOU WANPING
LOU MING

Special Consultants
SHAO HUAZE
LUN XUN

Project Director
WEI MINGXIANG

Project Coordinators
WEI LONGQUAN
LI DONG
ZHANG DECAI
SONG SHAOFU
LI QIANGUANG

Balloon Coordinator
XING ZHIHUA

Translators
YANG LINGENG
ZU YONGREN
HAN SHIWAN
WANG LEI
LI TIANLIN

Interpreters
WANG LEI
MING YALIN
QIAO HONG
WANG JUANJUAN
WANG WEI
ZHANG DONGSHAN

Photographers
GEORG GERSTER   Switzerland
WU SHOUZHUANG   China
JERRY YOUNG   UK
DAN BUDNIK   USA
PAUL LAU   Hong Kong

with
ZHOU WANPING   China
ZHOU YI   China
WEI MINGXIANG   China
LI QIANGUANG   China
GEORGE MITCHELL   USA
HARALD SUND   USA
CHE FU   China
WU JINSHENG   China

Cover
The mountains of Guilin.
JERRY YOUNG

Endpapers
Fish farms scattered around the fringes
of Lake Dianchi.
JERRY YOUNG

Pages 2-3
The Chess Playing Pavilion occupies
one of the summits of the sacred
Flowery Mountain, Shaanxi province.
PAUL LAU

Pages 4-5
Above the Li River, drifting between
the sugarloaf mountains of Guilin.
JERRY YOUNG

Page 6
In the loess lands of Shaanxi, erosion
has changed the face of the land
forever. WU SHOUZHUANG

Opposite page
A traffic jam develops on the Grand
Canal between Suzhou and Wuxi in
Jiangsu province. GEORG GERSTER

Pages 10-11
Rice fields near the village of Longqui
in central Sichuan .
HARALD SUND

Published in the United States of America in 1988
by The Knapp Press
5900 Wilshire Boulevard
Los Angeles, California 90036

Jointly produced by
INTERCONTINENTAL PUBLISHING CORPORATION LTD
69 Wyndham Street, 4/F, Hong Kong
Telex 83499 PPA HX; Fax 5-8101683
A member of the Weldon International Group of Companies
Sydney • Auckland • Hong Kong • London • Chicago

and

CHINA GREAT WALL PUBLISHING HOUSE
40 San Li He Road, Gan Jia Kou, Beijing, China

CHINA NATIONAL PUBLISHING INDUSTRY TRADING CORPORATION
504 An Hua Li, An Ding Men Wai, Beijing, China
PO Box 782, Beijing, China

© 1988 Intercontinental Publishing Corporation,
China Great Wall Publishing House
and China National Publishing Industry Trading Corporation

Library of Congress Cataloguing-in-Publication Data

Over China

Includes index
1. China — Description and travel — 1976 — Views.
I. Budnik, Dan. II. Sinclair, Kevin, 1942–
DS712.0875   1988   915.1'0022'2   88-9298

ISBN 0-89535-216-8

Designed by The Book Design Co, Sydney
Typeset by Keyset Phototype Pty Ltd, Sydney
Printed by Griffin Press Limited, Adelaide
Printed in Australia

A KEVIN WELDON/GWP & CNPITC PRODUCTION

CONVERSION CHART

Imperial to Metric units

CONVERSION CHART

Imperial to Metric units

1 inch = 25.4 mm
1 foot = 0.304 m
1 mile = 1.61 km

1 ton = 1.02 t

1 acre = 0.405 ha
1 square mile = 2.6 km²

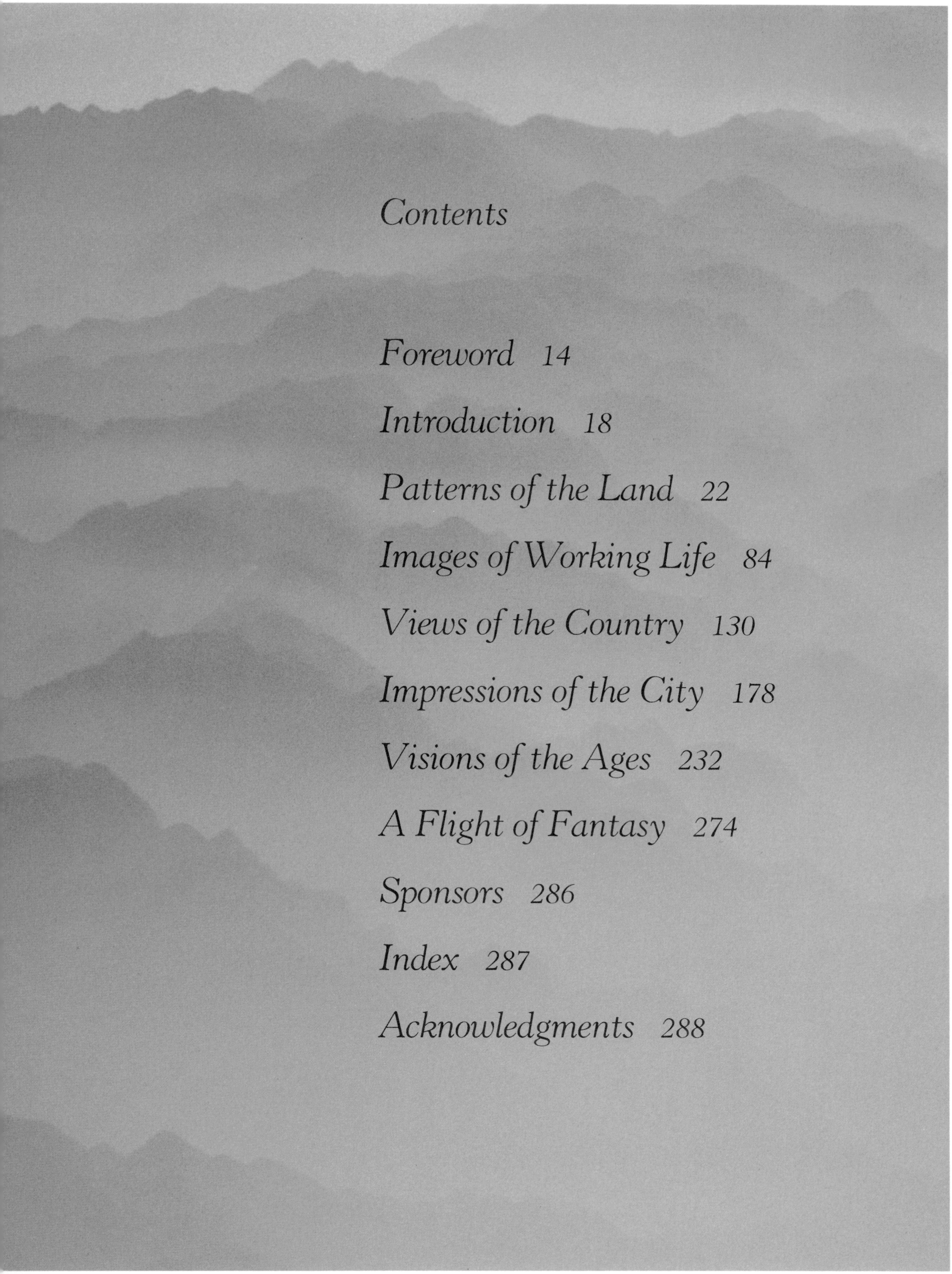

JERRY YOUNG

Contents

Foreword 14

Introduction 18

Patterns of the Land 22

Images of Working Life 84

Views of the Country 130

Impressions of the City 178

Visions of the Ages 232

A Flight of Fantasy 274

Sponsors 286

Index 287

Acknowledgments 288

FOREWORD

*B*etween 1933 and 1936 a German aviator, Wulf Diether, Graf von Castell (Count von Castell), flew over China to survey new domestic air routes to link China's major cities. This venture, which was the result of cooperation between a German airline and the Chinese national government, had commenced in 1930, and by the time the Count arrived in June 1933 two major routes had already been opened up. After his first flight, Diether was so impressed with the unusual forms of the Chinese landscape that he decided to capture it in photographs which were published in a book *Chinaflug* (China Flight) in 1938. 'I believe I have succeeded in getting material that shows the known in a new light — the greater perspective of aerial photographs — and which contain much that is completely unknown to others and that these [pictures] can serve to extend our knowledge of China.' This photograph was shot above the mountains in Zhejiang.

N O ONE, no Chinese, no foreigner, has ever seen the China that is spread before our eyes on the pages of *Over China*. This is a China lifted above the range of mortal eyes, a China that somehow inhabits a magical space just under the rim of heaven, a China of boundless distance, of lonely temples on bewitched mountains, of chessboard quadrants spanning dozens of leagues, a greener green than Ireland, with soil as black as the ace of spades.

This unearthly quality is not accidental; it is very Chinese. For three millennia the Chinese have called their country not China (that word derives from a nomadic tribe on China's northern marches) but the Middle Kingdom. The term did not define a realm lying somewhere between Russia and India but a land between Heaven and Earth, rather closer to Heaven than Earth.

Much has changed in China but that concept of a heavenly kingdom has not vanished. It is brought to our eyes in the portfolio of the *Zhongguo*, and its people, presented in this volume. *Over China* catches the essence of the vision that has been cherished by inhabitants of China for centuries, a vision long hidden by the dust and dirt of China's daily life. Each picture is illuminated by that Chinese intuition, each reflects the unique quality of a land with no parallel in global history.

Never before has this world been accessible — not because its quality could not be imagined but because until the development of modern technology, specifically the art of aerial photography and advanced color reproduction and printing, it just could not be done.

Any doubters can turn to a 40-year-old issue of the *National Geographic* magazine which reproduced photographs taken by an early German aviator, Captain Hans Korster, who spent some 4000 hours flying over China in the 1930s. Korster was a good aviator (his most advanced plane was a Ford trimotor) and photographer, but his pictures of China look as though they were taken from a high stepladder with a child's box camera.

Over China represents the climax of modern technology, combined with the artistry of some of the world's best photographers. Dr Georg Gerster of Switzerland practically invented aerial photography as an artform. He has flown hundreds of miles over China in hot-air balloons. His artistic talent for portraying China was first exhibited in the extravagant expedition (by the same partnership) which recaptured in pictures the 6000-mile Long March of Chairman Mao Zedong and his Red Army.

To the skills of Dr Gerster have been added those of Dan Budnik, the American photojournalist, the Englishman Jerry Young, and those of Wu Shouzhuang, China's premier aerial photographer. The Hong Kong photographer Paul Lau contributes photographs of the daily life of the Chinese people. This photographic artistry has been coupled with text by Kevin Sinclair, MBE, a student of China and her peoples.

The key to the success of this endeavor has been the collaboration of China's People's Liberation Army. Without the aid and cooperation of the Chinese army it would have been impossible for the photographers to travel by helicopter and fixed-wing plane and hot-air balloon some 20 000 miles through China's air space.

Never before has a work of this scope been attempted. Photographs were taken at 150 locations — the Silk Road, the Gobi Desert, the ricefields of central China, nomadic Inner Mongolia, the Great Wall, the great rivers, the cities of Shanghai, Nanjing and Beijing, the mountains of Yunnan, the remote deserts of Xinjiang. For the first time we see from the air the eternal beauty of China's fertile plains, the savage majesty of her cliffs, the torrents of her rivers, the remoteness of the back country — all the elements that have caused the Chinese to believe they live in a world apart. Theirs is the land of humanity's longest recorded historical experience, a land of unmatched art and treasure. No viewer of the Great Wall as seen by the cameras of *Over China* can doubt the awe with which it will be viewed by the first observer from distant space.

This volume is the second to be produced in partnership with the China National Publishing Corporation and the Great Wall Publishing House, a subsidiary of the PLA. The skills and insights gained in the first venture have flowered into this spectacular vision of China, the Middle Kingdom.

HARRISON SALISBURY

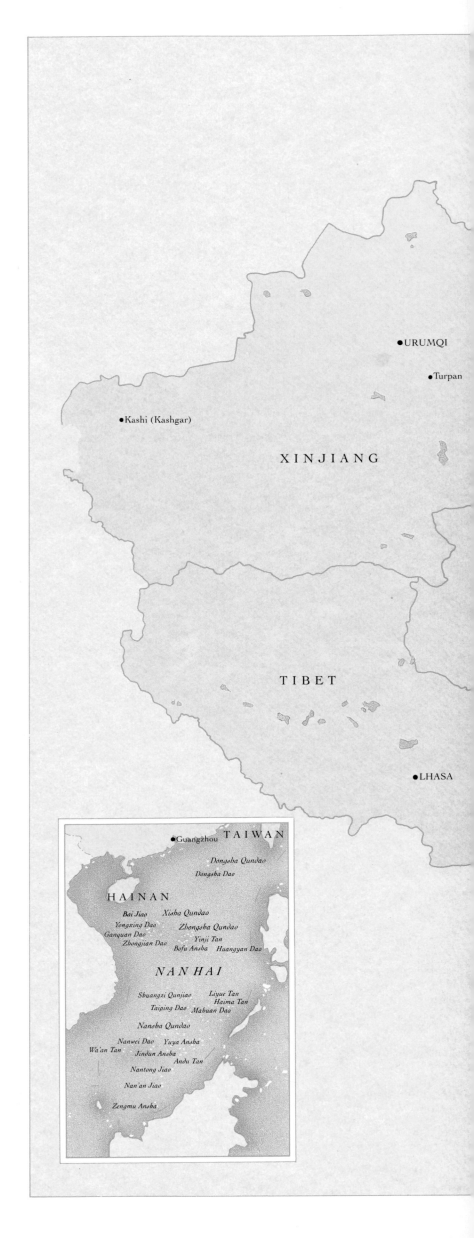

*D*aguang Park, with its many pavilions and flower gardens, is on the outskirts of Kunming, the capital of Yunnan province, a city renowned for its delightful climate.

INTRODUCTION

All under the sky are one family.

Li Jing, *The Book of Rites*, compiled by Dai Sheng and Dai De in the Han Dynasty 208BC–25AD

THROUGHOUT HISTORY the emperors of China have charged scholars to tabulate the wealth of the nation. The encyclopedic tome *The Tribute of Yu*, which itemised every stream, hill, town and source of economic wealth, was compiled more than fifteen centuries before William the Conqueror's Doomsday Book. The writ of the Dragon Throne ran over a land of enormous riches. Since that volume, more than nine thousand regional studies of China's geography have been written for scores of rulers, handbooks for tax collectors and scholars alike.

Our photographers have been able to approach China from a perspective very different from that of scholars who once tramped across every *mu* of the realm. With the aid of aircraft flown by pilots of the People's Liberation Army, the cameramen have soared and hovered above the landscape, photographing it from an angle previously unknown. China is larger than the United States with five times as many people, twice as large as Europe with double the population of that continent. The view from above illustrates how one-fifth of mankind feeds itself, provides shelter, and creates an agricultural economy as old as civilization.

What may look mundane from eye-level emerges as surprisingly exciting from above. The significance of the geometrical architecture of Daoist, Buddhist and Confucian temples can be grasped more simply from the air; the symmetry of courtyards and halls merges into a logical pattern.

Also revealed is the structure of the land. From the vantage point of a high-soaring kite, the valleys and hills, streams and rivers, roads and villages, all fall into sequence. The viewer can see how nature made the land, why rivers sought a path to the lowlands, how man has carved his initials into rice-terraced hillsides. In late afternoon, as the sun slants down sharply from the west, the aviator above the great dun-colored North China Plain can see unlikely shadows cast over the fields of wheat, rapeseed and barley. At high noon the land appears flat and featureless. But as dusk nears, shadows illuminate meandering patterns. These obscure, curving forms in the earth are illustrations from the ice ages showing where the Yellow River has changed its course time and again to disgorge silt into the Bohai Sea over a thousand miles of shifting coast.

The majesty of man can also be perceived easily from on high. Symmetrical humps and domes that from the surface appear to be natural hills are seen from the air to have rectangular patterns that nature could never devise. They mark the tombs of long-forgotten kings. Across the broad shoulders of the historic frontier the aerial observer can follow the seemingly endless folds of the Great Wall as that mightiest of fortifications pushes over loess crests and desert dunes. The ancient city walls, most of them now gone, can still be traced.

From the sky, tiny rice paddies give way to hillside tea plantations, to broad fields of wheat and barley, and then to the wide freedom of the steppes. From the

crammed coastal belt with the highest population densities on earth, the land stretches westward to the lonely ice plateaus where man is a stranger among the peaks. The most populous land on the planet also has untouched forested mountain ranges, deserts of stone and gravel, highland meadows barren but for occasional herds of yaks, and snows in which the Swiss Alps would be lost.

The Tibet–Qinghai plateau covers almost a million square miles, an area bigger than Western Europe excluding Scandinavia. Within this enormous swathe of the roof of the world, bleak but beautiful, there are very few signs of habitation. Wandering nomads pick out a living following their flocks of yak and sheep, much as their forefathers did for centuries. This is a geologically dramatic land. Here soar the world's highest peaks, Qomolangma (Everest) and Kanchenjunga. It is a land where rivers are born. Snaking down from the snows of Tibet and Qinghai are streams that will become the Salween and the Mekong, the Huanghe, and the mightiest of them all, the Yangtze.

The rivers and mountains further to the east have figured prominently in the poetry, art and culture of China. For well over twenty centuries, the five sacred Buddhist mountains of Tai, Emei, Jiuhua, Putao and Wutai have exerted a mystical hold over the people. As the aerial explorer soars in the wake of eagles past the peak of sacred Taishan, pagodas and pavilions emphasize the role such pinnacles play in the cultural bonds that so closely tie the Chinese to their land. The craving that takes tens of thousands of people every year to trek up the precipitous flanks of Taishan to the summit, there to spend a chilly night waiting to catch a glimpse of dawn, is an urge buried deep in the racial memory. There are strains of old religion, folk belief, and teachings of sages such as Confucius and Mencius, mixed into this regard for the rocky crests. Flying past these crags, bamboo-adorned, flanks clad with pine, pinnacles shrouded with mist, it is easy to see where poets for 3000 years have gained their inspiration.

The landscape painters of the past had to gain their view of the heavenly mountains from ground level. Schools of painters over the centuries tried mentally to elevate their perspective to the clouds, attempting to visualize the face of the land from the viewpoint of the gods. Our photographic artists have succeeded where the painters of the past could only strive in their imagination. They have looked at the land from a fresh viewpoint — from *Over China*.

*R*ising 6000 feet in spectacular, jagged beauty, the many peaks of Huashan in Shaanxi have for centuries been home to celebrated hermits, subject for artists, inspiration for poets. But ascending the Flowery Mountain is no easy task; the god Laojun in mythical times is said to have plowed an axe-like path across a sheer flank of a precipice using heavenly oxen.

PATTERNS OF THE LAND

*P*ainted with vivid colors from nature's palette, newly plowed fields contrast with ripening crops. Yunnan's moist warm climate is perfect for cultivating rice and growing tropical fruits.

PATTERNS OF THE LAND

If you do not scale the high hill, you cannot view the plain.

Old peasant folklore

Previous pages

*I*nspiration for a thousand painters, the limestone crags of Guilin seem to march off endlessly into the mists of summer.

THROUGH A CAMERA LENS mounted on a Chinese satellite spinning high above the earth, the geography of China, 3.7 million square miles, unfolds like a panoramic painting. It is no accident that the landscape has been likened to a huge three-tiered staircase dropping from the serried mountain ranges down to the plateaus and high steppes, finally descending to the hills and plains where live most of the country's huge population.

From the Black Dragon River looping over the frigid northeastern plains down to the fronds of South Sands Island in the South China Sea is a distance of 3410 miles. From the crests of the lonely Pamirs in Central Asia to the East China Sea is 3100 miles. As the noon sun shines in Beijing, dawn is breaking on the Central Asian caravanserai city of Kashi (Kashgar). Within this enormous confine is a nation that contains almost every geographical feature on earth.

As the circling satellite spins toward the Asian mainland, it first spots the outcrops girdling the coast — the two major islands of Taiwan and Hainan and the 5000 smaller offshore isles. Then the moving satellite brings into view the rich coastal plains with their fertile river deltas and crowded valleys.

The land rises. In the south it is a sudden process, the wooded hills breaking from the plains close to the coast, growing range upon range until they march off into the misty tribal highlands of Guizhou and Yunnan provinces. To the north the earth climbs more gradually, tilting slowly upward from the plains to the first step of the geographical ladder that takes the viewer onto the savagely eroded loess highlands of Shanxi and Shaanxi. Around the entire southwestern arc of the nation, the view from the satellite shows a gleaming shield of ice and snow where the mighty Himalayas embrace Tibet.

From this massive mountain strongpoint, the land drops north to the arid plains of Xinjiang and Inner Mongolia. This is a place where running waters die as they dwindle to a trickle and disappear damply into the sands of the Gobi and Taklimakan deserts. Divided by the peaks of the Mountains of Heaven, Xinjiang is part steppe, part desert. The Bogda Mountains plunge down into the Turpan Depression, where the surface of Lake Aydingkol glitters like a sapphire 500 feet below sea level.

Spreading north and east of Xinjiang like a scimitar are the grasslands and steppes of Inner Mongolia. Here the Khans once rode to horror and bloody glory, and here today their descendants ride still. In great cities of steel and coal, like the industrial metropolis of Baotou, men and women drag out the hidden riches of the earth. But on most of Mongolia's endless prairies the tents of herdsmen are a more common sight.

At the bottom of the geographer's staircase are the lowlands. To the north is the blacksoil plain of the northeast whose natural fertility yields impressive crops in the short summers and whose mineral wealth has turned many of its cities into

major foundries. From the air, golden fields of wheat stretch to the horizon where factory chimneys tower above steelworks. The plains roll south, and the land turns yellow as the Huanghe continuously dumps heavy layers of silt. Over a million years the river has carried its rich load from the loess lands to deposit a layer hundreds of feet thick over the North China Plain. The river made the entire province of Henan, much of Shandong, Hebei, Anhui and Jiangsu. From this heartland the satellite camera sweeps further south to the broad flood of the Yangtze and its immensely rich valley.

The southern arc of China's coastal provinces is a geological jigsaw puzzle. The Pearl slashes like a muddy highway down from Guangxi to its delta. A lacework of rivers and streams tumble through limestone karsts and granite hills to the jagged coasts where ancient trading ports like Xiamen and Wenzhou, Shantou and Zhanjiang are enclosed in snug natural harbors against the fury of the typhoons that every year batter this coastline. Inland, the jumbled hills are cut by a million waterways. Along every bank the paddies stretch eternally green.

Rivers were the basis of earliest Chinese life. Chinese civilization itself sprang from the irrigated soil somewhere near where the Huai River joins the Huanghe. On the outskirts of the modern metropolis of Xi'an, archeologists have excavated a prosperous farming village that 6000 years ago grew up on the banks of a small stream. Geographers claim that China has 51 500 rivers with a total length of 240 900 miles. These days, the streams and rivers that tumble down from the central massifs of Asia find their headlong plunge broken periodically by dams.

The human manipulation of the waters of China, which can be seen on almost every flight, is nothing new. It has been going on for at least five thousand years, since the legendary emperor Yu the Great is said to have tamed the Yellow River. Flying over Jiangsu province, China's richest, one can see the most spectacular and famous of man's attempts to mold nature to his will, the arrow-straight waterway of the Grand Canal. Grand it is indeed, as Marco Polo and other foreigners have marveled for centuries. When Polo traveled along the canal by barge as Mongol invaders put the finishing touches on this majestic project, much of the waterway was already venerable.

Few aerial sights are as dramatic as the meeting place of land and sea. The coastline, 11 180 miles long from the Korean border port of Dandong down to the Gulf of Tonkin in Guanxi, washes shores that range from saltmarshes to beaches framed with tropical palms — as well as ports that boast steel cranes, miles of concrete piers, railheads and highways, and container terminals. The romance of man and sea is not entirely wiped out by progress; low-slung junks, with eyes painted warily on the bows, still set sail in the China Seas.

*T*wisted granite folds thrust up through the earth's crust. The rocky skeleton of the Qinghai highlands is often more than 13 000 feet above sea level.

*M*ost of the vast southwestern province of Tibet consists of high barren mountains sprawling over a rolling plateau 13 000 feet above sea level. Sparsely settled by roving bands of nomadic herdsmen and a few farmers who raise millet, Tibet was for centuries a closed land ruled by feudal lamas. Even today, the mineral resources of the region have been scarcely scratched by development. Above, the icy peaks of nameless Tibetan mountains emerge from the clouds in this highest of all China's provinces. Stretching 1500 miles from east to west, in a belt 150 miles wide, the mighty ranges gird the southern rim of Tibet. At right, the gentler contours of the plateau stretch seemingly endlessly across the land.

Overleaf

*B*lanketed by thick morning clouds, most of the fabled peaks of Huangshan in Anhui are hidden from those who have climbed the highest pinnacles to observe the dawn. Inspiration for artists for centuries, the Yellow Mountain is studded with scenery that can be seen in many a painting in national galleries.

*A*lmost every pinnacle has its legend in the eroded natural sculpture gallery of the Stone Forest of Yunnan. The Sanyi minority people, for whom the area is home, trace their descent to a mythical couple who fled oppressive landlords to take shelter amid the craggy ramparts. Formed by erosion over a period estimated by geologists as 200 million years, the spectacular limestone karsts resemble birds, beasts and demons, with rocks bearing names like 'Phoenix Preening its Feathers.'

JERRY YOUNG

GEORG GERSTER

A blazing natural signpost on the Silk
Road, the Flaming Mountains of the
Turpan Depression guide travelers toward
cool oases where dates, grapes and melons
await. Hot air rushes along the cliff face and
blows on to travelers with furnace heat.
When the sun's rays strike the mountain
slopes at the right angle, the red cliffs glow
as though on fire.

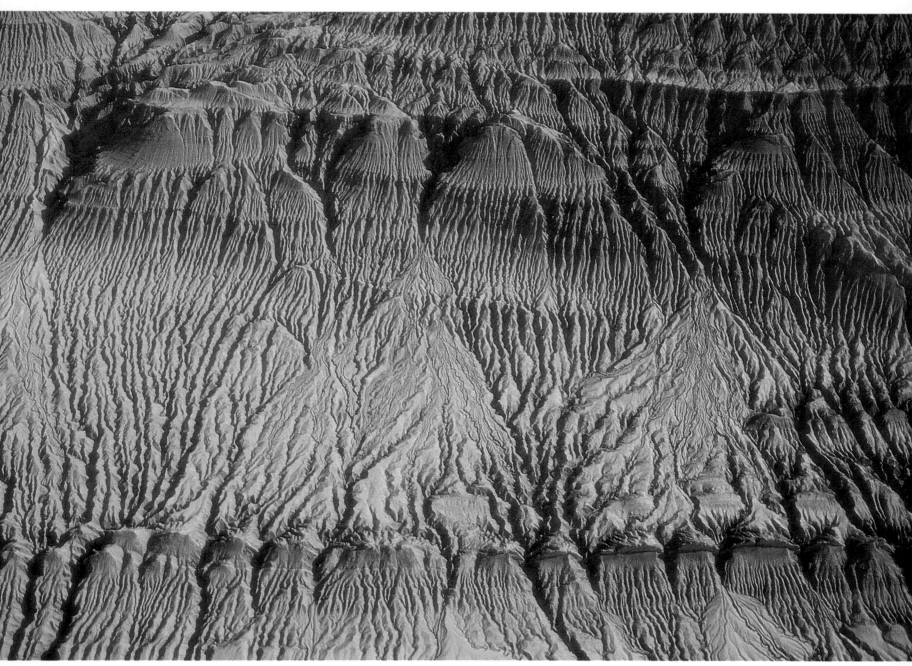

GEORG GERSTER

*T*he weathered face of the Flaming
Mountains of Xinjiang. Although harsh
climatic conditions make much of Xinjiang
useless for agriculture, geologists believe
that many rare and valuable minerals are
locked in the earth. In mythology,
wandering Tang Dynasty monk Xuan
Zhuang passed this way to bring the
Buddhist scriptures from India.

GEORG GERSTER

GEORG GERSTER

*E*mperors of old built the Great Wall to safeguard China from barbarians. Today, more effectively, the nation has erected a Green Wall to protect farmland and pastures from encroaching deserts. In a wide band stretching across the arid lands of north and west, more than 650 million acres of land has been planted with trees. The green arc sweeps across eleven provinces and autonomous regions from Heilongjiang to Xinjiang, providing windbreaks that stop the sand dunes from taking over valuable agricultural land. Here in Mongolia, crusted dunes of sand near Bikeqi meet newly planted vegetation.

*I*n Inner Mongolia there is a never-ending battle to farm the land. The loess plateau, victim to cruel erosion, is being constantly attacked by relentless nature.

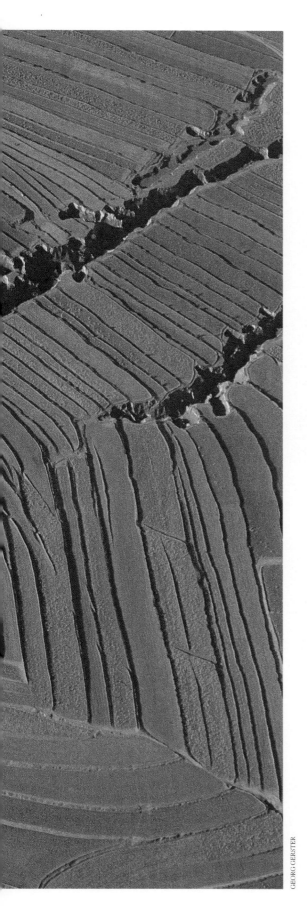

GEORG GERSTER

GEORG GERSTER

A patchwork of wheat, vegetables, oilseed and newly plowed fields north of the Mongolian capital of Hohhot hints at the new agricultural wealth of the plains. Once home to nomadic horsemen, Mongolia now grows rich on settled agriculture and increasing industrialization.

*T*erraces climb up steep hillsides to protect Mongolian farmland from further erosion. Gullies slice into the land like wounds inflicted by a giant axeman.

WU SHOUZHUANG

*B*earing a heavier load of silt than any
other waterway in the world, the Yellow
River dumps billions of tons of earth on its
bed as it courses through the loess region.
The silt forms a platform on which the
river rises, until the waterway is high above
the level of surrounding plains. When
floodwaters peak and the torrent breaks its
banks, the Yellow River earns its name of
'China's Sorrow.' Today's planners claim
they have achieved a proud objective; they
have tamed the Huanghe.

GEORG GERSTER

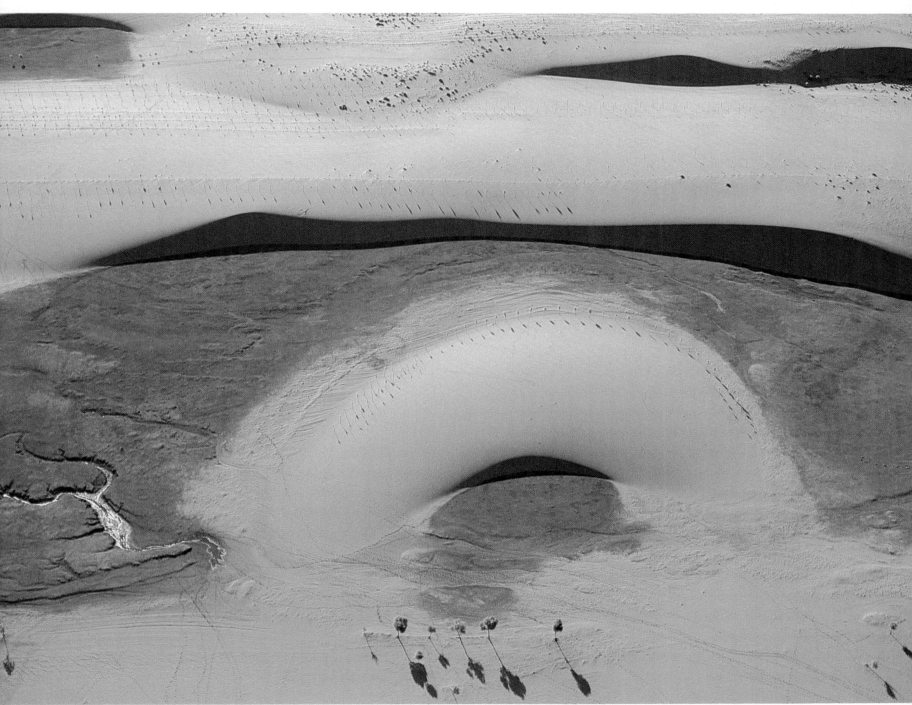

WU SHOUZHUANG

*C*reated by the winds of Central Asia, the sand dunes of the Tengger Desert march across Mongolia and into the Ningxia Autonomous Region. The fourth-largest desert in China, the Tengger covers an area as large as Taiwan. The dunes constantly encroach upon the Mongolian farmland, where a ceaseless battle is waged between man and nature for control of the landscape.

Previous pages

*O*nly a third of Liaoning's 57 700 square miles can be used for farming; much of the province is covered by wild northern mountain forests. Land under the plow produces notable crops of cotton, peanuts, sorghum and maize. Orchards provide the juiciest apples in China and plump pears that make the name of Liaoning synonymous with temperate fruit. As well as valuable timber, the extensive forests are the source of herbs such as precious ginseng and deer antlers prized by traditional doctors as powerful potions.

*W*hen the sun of Xinjiang strikes the face of the Flaming Mountains, the etched cliffs glow a bold scarlet hue. Ancient wanderers pushing westward into the unknown lands of Central Asia wrote that reflected heat from the cliffs blasted the desert floor as though from a furnace.

WU SHOUZHUANG

GEORG GERSTER

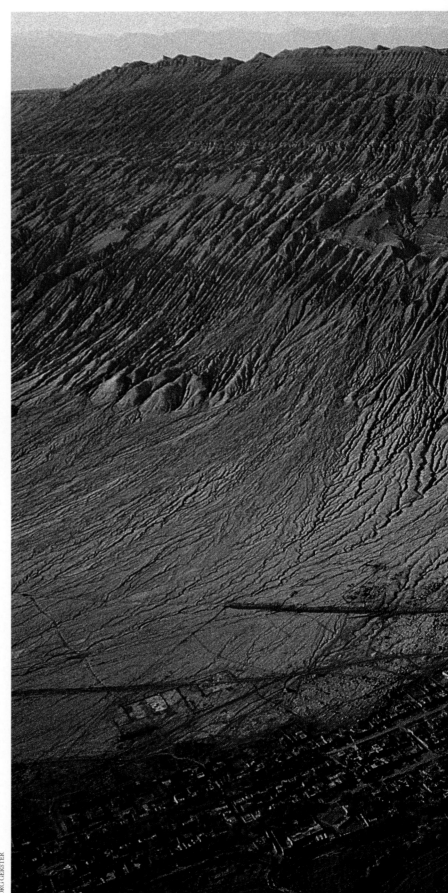

GEORG GERSTER

*C*hina's Wild West, Xinjiang's wide spaces are home to nomads. Kazakhs, Uygurs and other horsemen ride these dusty plains across an area bigger than Western Europe. Long disputed by many emperors, Xinjiang was the frontier of empire for 2000 years, sometimes under rule of the Dragon Throne, sometimes occupied by usurpers, often under the sway of local warlords or lawless tribesmen. This sprawling province straddles the Central Asian landmass. A land of many peoples, it provided the historic route between China and the West.

*T*he grapes and melons of Xinjiang were fruits that men dreamed of as they trudged the Central Asian deserts of the Silk Road. Once they reached the welcome oasis towns of Xinjiang, they could rest their pack animals and relax in the orchards of ancient trading towns like Turpan.

Almost lost in the immensity of Tibet's expansive landscape, the tents of nomadic herdsmen cluster under the flank of a rearing mountain at Damxung. This uncommonly large gathering of tribesmen was occasion for a grasslands festival.

PAUL LAU

WU SHOUZHUANG

*T*he stark Qiling Ranges, which stretch from the Gansu–Qinghai border across north to southeast China, are the major reason for significant climatic variation. Peaks over 9000 feet prevent moist summer winds from taking rain to the arid northwest. The mountains also trap cold Siberian airstreams and stop them from sweeping from the frigid north during icebox winters. Mount Qilian in western Gansu soars 16 000 feet above dun-shaded, knife-edged foothills.

Right

*L*ong a subject of legend but little known to the Chinese of the lowlands, the Lake of Heaven nestles amid the peaks of the Xinjiang alps. Ancient folklore tells of a magic peach tree that gave fruit once every thousand years. When the sacred crop was picked, immortals were invited to banquet on the shores of the lake by the Mother of the Western Skies. The Mountains of Heaven stretch an imposing 1200 miles from east to west through the center of Xinjiang, cutting the province in half. Now linked to Urumqi 30 miles away by a tortuous road that snakes up cliff-like spurs, the long-isolated Lake of Heaven is a newly discovered destination for tourists.

GEORG GERSTER

*T*he harsh landscape of Xinjiang has been
fought over by many armies. Providing
both a link and a buffer between China and
Central Asia, the province was
administered during the Han Dynasty.
Fields in this dry and dusty province spring
to life only with irrigation.

A place of legend, the Huashan mountains
in Shaanxi province are known as a haven
for gods, a place of respite for heavenly
lovers. Today, hundreds of thousands of
visitors yearly climb the steep cliffs to catch
a glimpse of the dawn from such vantage
points as the tiny plateau named Peak of
the Morning Sun.

GEORG GERSTER

*A*mid the hills of Hebei, precious water
swirls and curves like a dragon as it builds
up behind a dam on the Miyun River north
of Beijing. Building dams is a priority for
planners in every area of the nation. The
north, drier and with less reliable rainfall
than the wetter southern provinces, makes
great efforts to preserve falls from
infrequent rains.

GEORG GERSTER

*T*he Miyun reservoir is full to the brim
after unusual heavy rain, with the rising
water encroaching on nearby fields. The
water held in dams such as this provides a
source of power for turbines as well as a
secure supply for irrigation.

Overleaf

*G*ently contoured to hold the water needed
to nurture the rice crop, dry-season fields
near the town of Dangyang in Hubei have
been drained for the harvest. With the next
rains, the mud-walled dykes will brim
again, ready for another transplanting of
rice seedlings.

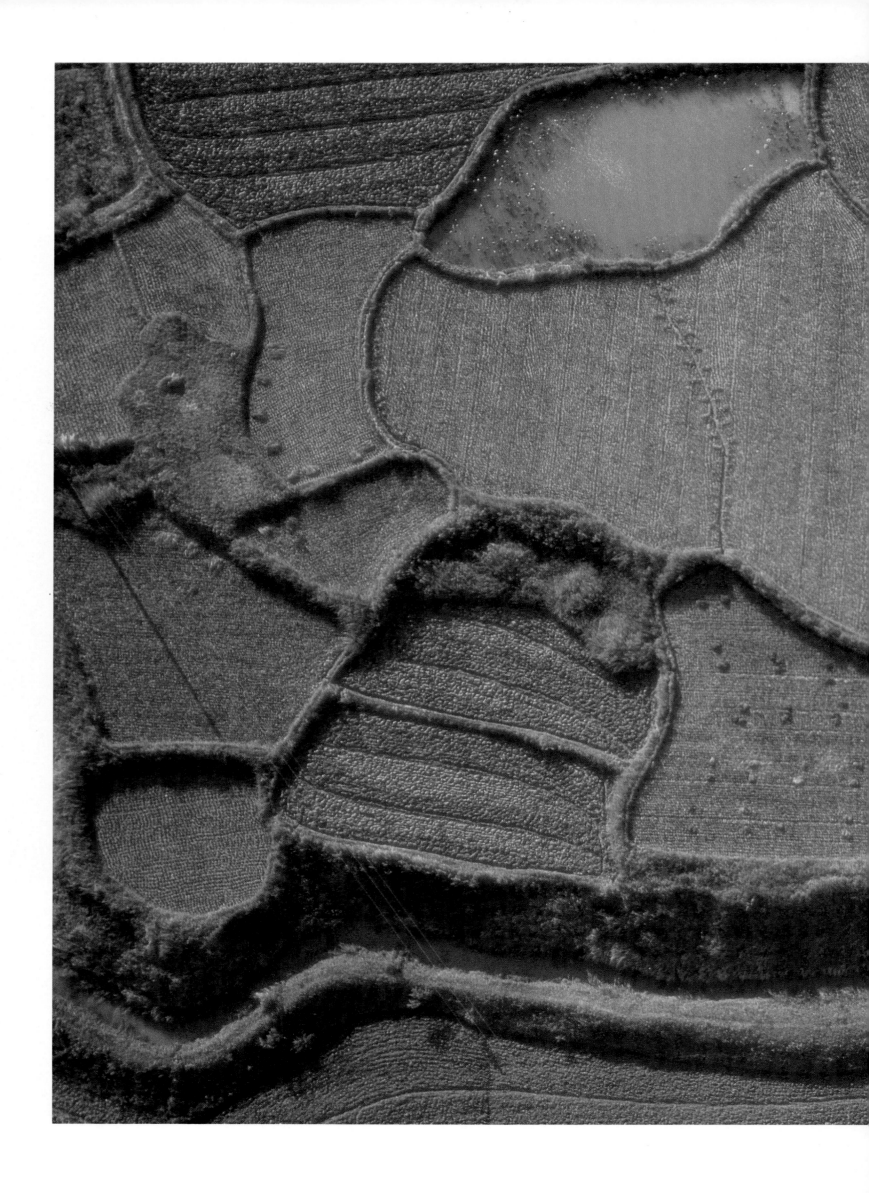

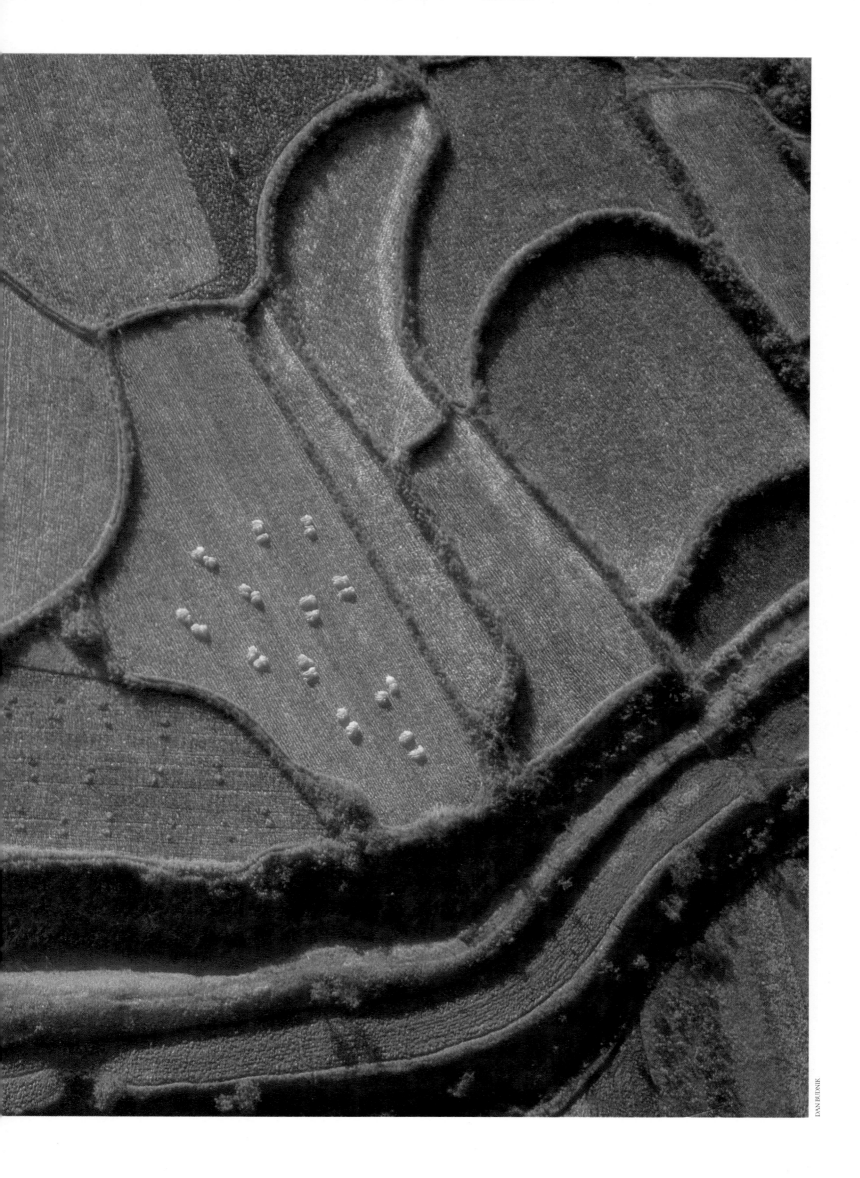

GEORG GERSTER

GEORG GERSTER

*T*he mountain ranges of Xinjiang cover huge areas. This largely underpopulated autonomous region in the northwest is home to many Islamic minorities.

*F*ormed from red sandstone eroded by wind and enormous temperature variations which see summer mercury levels reach well over 100 degrees Fahrenheit, the Flaming Mountains of Xinjiang rise from the low flatlands of the Turpan Depression. Man finds little solace in this blistering lunar landscape.

WU SHOUZHUANG

*S*carred by gullies, sculpted by erosion, the hills of Gansu are stark testaments to the relentless force of nature.

*B*ald hills of Qinghai and Gansu will soon be covered with the plush greenery of pine, larch, birch and other hardy trees. Pockmarked by terrace works and hand-dug holes meant to harbor young trees, the steep eroded uplands are seeded from the air, part of a constant campaign to clothe the earth with a protective cover of vegetation. Since 1949, agricultural planners boast, state-encouraged afforestation programs have doubled the size of China's woodlands, helping to stem erosion and providing investment for future timber industries.

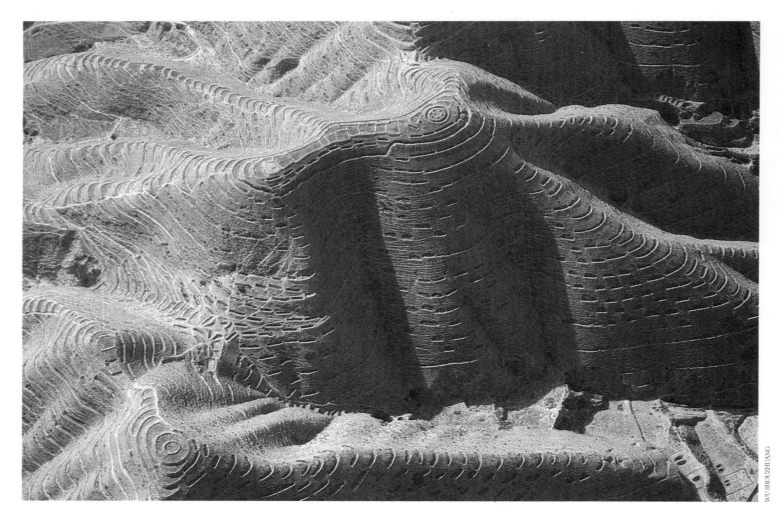

WU SHOUZHUANG

WU SHOUZHUANG

*I*n the arid foothills of the eastern Qinghai highlands, a mighty viaduct carries the main railway line from Xining to Lanzhou over a tributary of the Huanghe.

*Y*unnan means 'Beneath the Clouds,' and under the haze China's most southwesterly province is a land of seemingly endless hills populated by a bewildering twenty-three nationalities. The province is rich in rivers, and planners pin hope for development on harnessing hydroelectric power.

Below

*S*naking through the Yunnan valleys, one of the many rivers that dissect the jagged southwestern ranges shines through the eternal mists. Annual rainfall here measures up to 70 inches, most of which falls in the cooler months. But in these tropical valleys there is no winter, and the farmers of Yunnan reap three crops a year.

JERRY YOUNG

JERRY YOUNG

GEORG GERSTER

*F*ish farms encroach onto Lake Tai
between Wuxi and Suzhou. Hailed as a
Chinese version of a Garden of Eden, the
area is famed for its freshwater delicacies.

A rare water-rich part of Gansu, a small
tributary of the Daxia River flows into a
lake. Reflecting silver sheens, the waters
bring prosperity to farmers who raise yaks,
goats and cattle on surrounding plains.

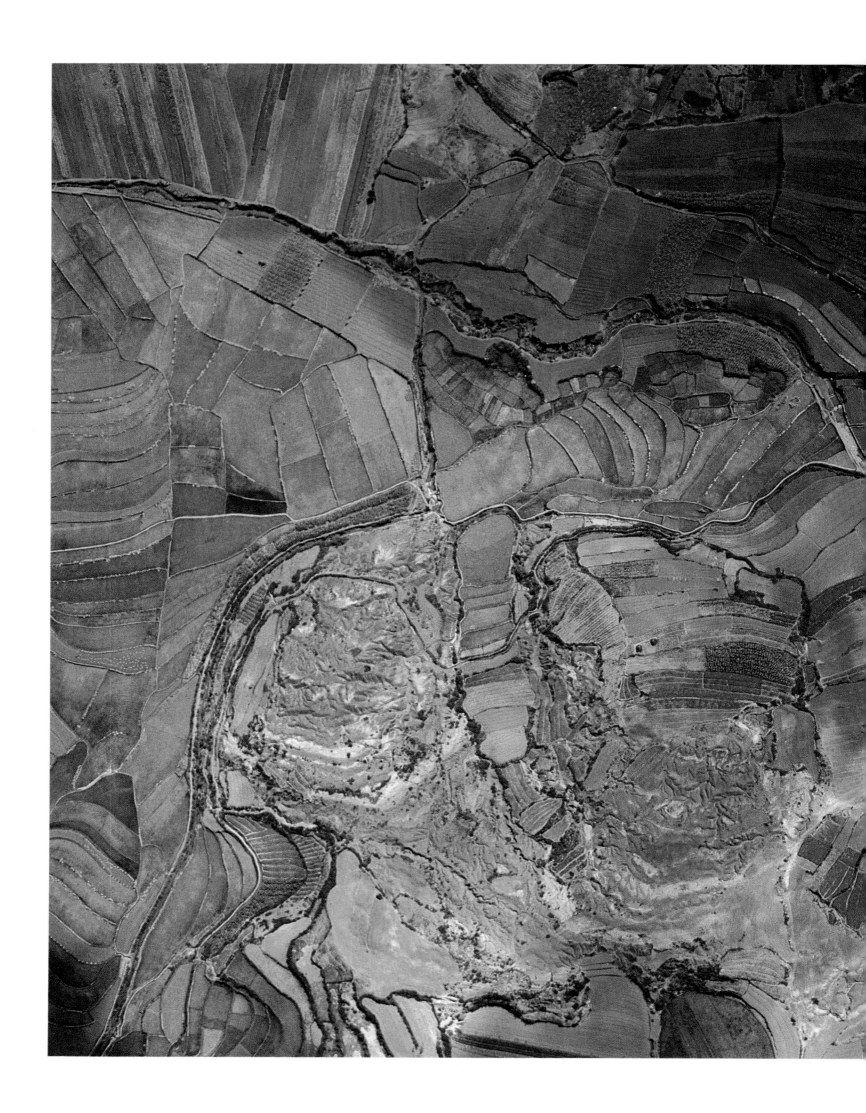

JERRY YOUNG

Previous pages

Golden reflections from fishponds outside Guangzhou hint at the wealth peasants harvest from these warm waters. Profitable crops of freshwater fish are scooped from the ponds, loaded into big floating tanks and swiftly barged 80 miles down the Pearl River to the gourmet restaurants of Hong Kong. Live fish fetch high prices from discriminating diners.

Nature has been kind indeed to the southwest. The climate is mild, rainfall is generous and reliable, the earth is fertile. Throughout history the people of China have cared for this land with skill, extracting ample benefits from its produce. In Sichuan and Yunnan, villagers live among some of the most spectacular scenery in the nation.

WUSHOUZHUANG

*H*ome to Muslims of many races, Ningxia Hui Autonomous Region has four million people in 25 500 square miles. Half follow the teachings of Islam; others in this ethnic melting pot are Han, Manchu, Mongol and Tibetan. The Great Wall and the Yellow River run in parallel across the land, and comprehensive water conservation and irrigation schemes now allow farmers to grow rice on their paddyfields in addition to such traditional crops as wolfberry, licorice and edible moss.

WU SHOUZHUANG

*T*he mud-loaded Huanghe runs through beds of silt as it curves across Gansu. Much of the landscape of the north is the same ochre hue. Winds bring endless loads of dun-colored dust to add to the loess plateau; summer rains wash topsoil into streams which carry it down to add to the yellow flood of the great river.

WU SHOUZHUANG

*L*ong held to be the poorest province in the land, Gansu strives to overcome its reputation for poverty. Verging on desert, dry cropland carefully farmed can produce wheat and millet. Fields bald after recent harvesting are dotted with stacked straw which will be used for animal fodder in the long winter or as fuel to keep the bitter cold out of farmers' homes.

*A*glow in the brief summer of a climate that offers only 120 frost-free days a year, fields of Heilongjiang hold promise of healthy harvests. Farmers accustomed to the sudden arrival of savage autumn frosts know that they must harvest their crops before snow blankets the land for six months and the earth freezes solid. But the hot, humid summers with long days of sunshine mean that storehouses are usually safely filled before the first icicles plunge the most northerly province into winter.

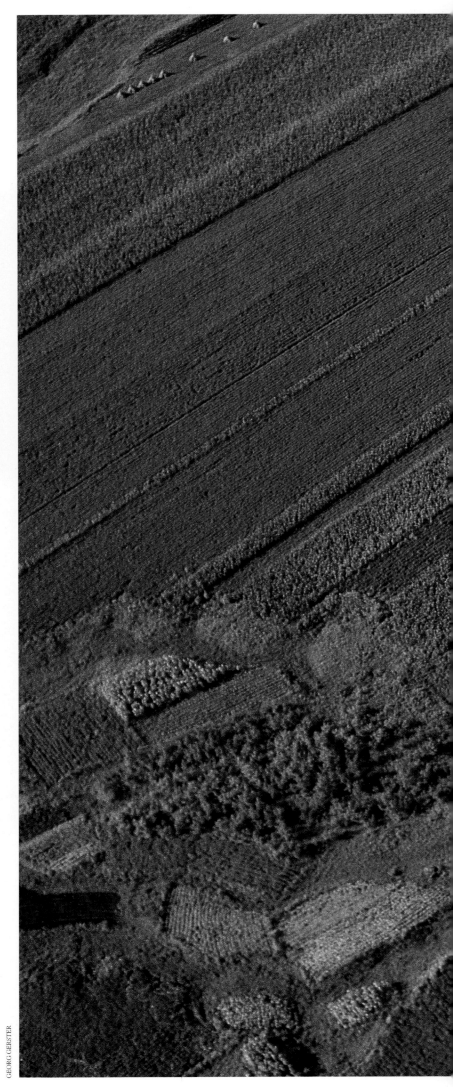

GEORG GERSTER

JERRY YOUNG

*L*ike an abstract painting, fields and dykes merge into an endless pattern in the fields outside Kunming.

*O*utside the city proper, Shanghai is rimmed by farmlands. Market gardeners take advantage of new economic regulations that allow them to sell surplus crops, and concentrate on high-value produce such as flowers and tasty vegetables for traditional culinary treats.

GEORG GERSTER

IMAGES OF WORKING LIFE

similarly being reformed in a bid to make them more competitive and efficient. Factory directors have been given greater responsibilities and are more accountable for profits and losses. In some cases the director now has the power to hire, fire, and set wages for workers. There are plans to set up a civil service to break down the current cadre system. The reforms have also allowed enterprising people to establish their own businesses. In the past decade privately run roadside stalls, restaurants, tailors, hairdressers and even coal mines have been opened up.

The reorganization of the economy has led to an industrial renaissance. In a decade, with the permission of the Chinese government, and fueled in part by joint-venture projects financed by Hong Kong, American, Japanese, Australian and European investors, China has branched out into fields more sophisticated, more ambitious, than in all its long history. Who would have believed, for instance, in 1978 that the United States would be chartering China's Long March 111 rockets to put American satellites into orbit? The move into agricultural, industrial, energy and transportation developments, consumer manufacturing, science and technology has made China self-sufficient in many areas and a major exporter of material and products ranging from oil to motor vehicles, clothing and furniture.

Motor vehicles are one visible standard of progress. Before 1949 there was not a single vehicle made in China; by 1957 the fledgling Number One Motor Vehicle factory in Jilin province was putting out 7900 vehicles a year. In 1980 China produced 222 000 trucks, cars, lorries and motorbikes (plus an additional 300 000 tractors); and by 1987 no fewer than 472 000 vehicles came off the assembly lines at plants all over the country.

The people of China have always valued the worth of work. The survival of not only the individual but of the whole family and the village has depended on the discipline of working together for the common good. Now that many Chinese have enough to feed and clothe themselves and their families, some are beginning to explore the hitherto unknown possibilities of leisure time.

*T*he solid brick houses of the industrial province of Jilin are provided by factories like this, which use the abundant local coal to fire the bricks.

*B*ridge-building at Shantou. The ancient
port city on the Guangdong coast is home
to the distinctive Xin Chao people, in the
past a widely scattered band of traders,
merchants, seamen and adventurers who
are now settled all over Southeast Asia.

91

*A*n October sunset over the Pearl River at Guangzhou, the most important industrial and foreign trade center in southern China. Since the early sixteenth century the city — then known as Canton — has been a trading center with the West, first with the Portuguese, then the Spanish, Dutch, British, French and Americans. In recent years Guangzhou has become the most prosperous city under China's open-to-the-outside-world policy.

*S*ails aloft to catch the morning breeze, junks glide over a burnished sea out from Shantou harbor to the fishing grounds.

DAN BUDNIK

*I*n the muddy shallows of the Huanghe in Shandong, fishermen tend their nets. A back-breaking task, icy in the long northern winters, it pays rich dividends. Fish feeling their way through the silt-laden waters are guided by the nets into traps.

*S*himmering across the placid surface of Lake Dianchi, nets cover fish farms that hold a rich freshwater harvest of carp and perch. Fishermen's shelters sit on stilts in the shallows, providing a resting place for those who feed the fish and care for the underwater cages that hold the crop.

HARALD SUND

*T*he day's work done, a fisherman sculls his way home over the placid River Li at Guilin. His craft stout bamboos lashed together with flax, his equipment a gape-mouthed net, the fisherman uses techniques unchanged for centuries.

Previous pages

*S*ecured tightly to the shore of lotus-covered Lake Dianchi near Kunming, a fleet of ferries awaits passengers. The vessels take farmers to and from their homes and provide sightseeing trips on the lake for tourists.

*L*ake Tai, fulcrum of the Grand Canal near Wuxi in Jiangsu, provides natural harvest grounds for fishermen. Developments in aquaculture and modern techniques of artificially breeding and raising fish bring a more certain livelihood to fishing families in the region.

GEORG GERSTER

JERRY YOUNG

*C*rops flourish in the tropic humidity of Yunnan province alongside Lake Dianchi, China's sixth-largest freshwater lake. Here, farmers tend neat fields that will provide food for the markets in the nearby provincial capital of Kunming.

DAN BUDNIK

*C*anny Shandong peasants use passing trucks and buses as part of the harvesting process on this road near Confucius' birthplace at Qufu. Winnowing the grain is an exhausting task, and by spreading the chaff on the roadway the farmers use passing vehicles to help do the job. Corn is also laid out on the hot concrete to speed the drying process needed before the ears can be stacked away for winter use.

Previous pages

*V*erdant under the tropic sun of Jiangxi's summer, crops near Ruijin are ready to harvest. The capital, Nanchang, is renowned as one of the five furnaces of China, named for its blasting combination of humidity and heat. With an annual rainfall of 80 inches there is no need for local farmers to irrigate their fields.

GEORG GERSTER

*C*hina's most northerly province, Heilongjiang has a savage continental climate. Winters are long and cold, and for half the year the ground is frozen solid. But this is a land of great natural wealth. Timber from Heilongjiang's huge natural forests provides building material for much of the nation. Most of China's paper is also produced from the forests of the far north, and these stacks of timber will go to a nearby pulp factory.

*T*hrough many dynasties, officials imposed heavy taxes on salt. It was an easy way to raise money; the salt monopoly levied harsh imposts on a basic product. Although most salt produced in China today comes from the sea, the country has proven reserves of 100 billion tons of the mineral in inland lakes and wells. Far inland in Xinjiang, local producers pump salt from wells. Moisture in the solution soon evaporates in the dry climate, leaving pure deposits for collection.

GEORG GERSTER

*O*n the fertile black soil of Heilongjiang, Friendship Farm is a model community that sets the standards for regional development. The province has vast wealth, much of it untapped. With 21 million acres of cultivated land, it produces enormous crops of soya bean, maize, wheat, sorghum, flax and sunflower seed on farms which are huge by the standards of the south. Once popularly known as 'the great northern wilderness,' Heilongjiang is now acclaimed as 'the great northern granary.' With 10 million acres of forest land, timber is a natural resource that helps propel Heilongjiang toward rapid development.

Over China

GEORG GERSTER

*L*ike ideographs of early writings from the
first dynasties, swirling lines of harvested
crops in Hebei fields seem to send a
message from earth to sky.

*N*eatly patterned, straw from a cleared
Hebei wheatfield is bundled for removal.
Flood control measures in recent decades
have dramatically improved harvests, and
arable cropland now under the plow has
grown to more than 16.5 million acres. A
major cotton and grain producer, Hebei
grows millet, maize and sorghum as well as
significant wheat crops. Its pears, chestnuts
and grapes are renowned delicacies, and the
peaches of Shenzhou farms have inspired
poets as well as gourmets.

GEORG GERSTER

GEORG GERSTER

*D*warfed by building blocks cut from a quarry in Sichuan, workers hack into a mountainside to extract more material. The rock is used for local building projects.

A frenzy of building is changing the face of many a Chinese city. Fueled partly by an unprecedented tourist boom, mostly because of the new economic policies that have given China's economy fresh impetus, foundations are being laid that will see modern high-rise structures dominate old skylines. In the former capital of Nanjing, the cityscape changes swiftly.

GEORG GERSTER

JERRY YOUNG

*T*hroughout China, brickworks are a sign of booming construction. New homes, factories and public buildings are commonly built of brick. Although the building materials industry has grown 11.5 per cent annually in recent years, it has not managed to keep pace with demand. Nationwide, there are almost 50 000 factories making bricks, cement and other materials needed to build a new China. Nevertheless, brickworks like this one on the outskirts of Beijing's expanding suburbs are working overtime to meet demand.

GEORG GERSTER

*A*n industrial foundry, Heilongjiang boasts
14 300 mining and manufacturing
concerns with 2.8 million workers. Copper,
lead, zinc, silver, cobalt, molybdenum,
bismuth and other riches are mined.
Geologists estimate that good-quality coal
reserves of 9000 million tons lie beneath
the province — fuel for chemical, paper,
steel and machinery factories. In one of the
most highly industrialized of all provinces,
about a third of Heilongjiang's 35 million
people live in big cities. Workers in this
brickworks on the banks of the navigable
Mudan River help to provide raw materials
for new industrial facilities.

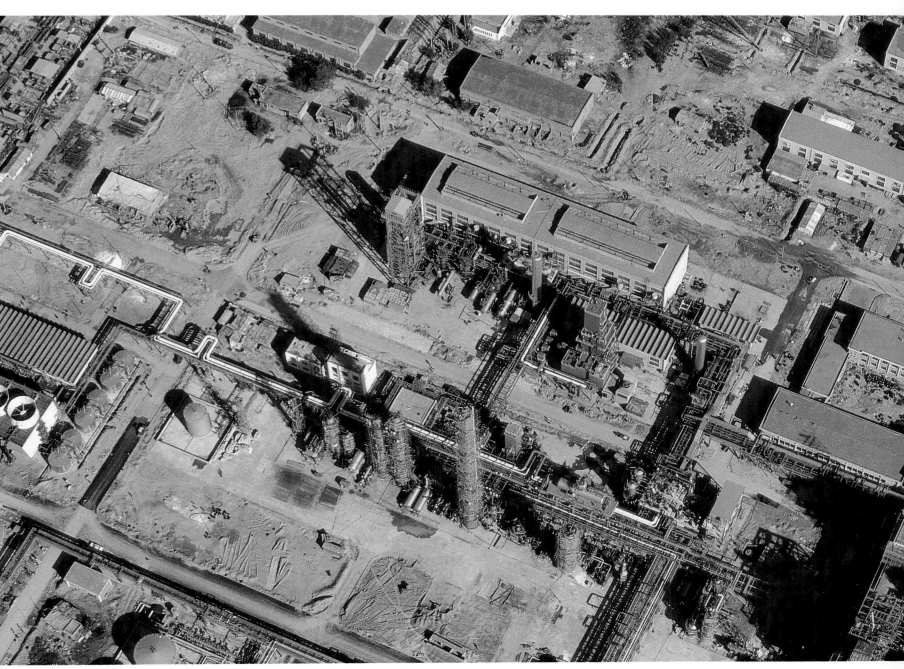

WU SHOUZHUANG

*L*ong backward and cursed by poverty, Ningxia is stirring economically. Skilled workers from other provinces are now helping to extract some of Ningxia's mineral wealth from the ground. This petrochemical plant will aid farmers by producing needed fertilizer and will help provincial planners by boosting funds needed to fuel future exploitation of phosphorus, gypsum and oil.

*J*ust as they opened up the American
West, so did the railways help to develop
the vast plains of China's northeast. From this
marshalling yard at Jiamusi in Heilongjiang
province, locomotives are dispatched to
haul trains throughout the region.

*T*he railway station in Turpan is a vital
hub on the long line that connects the
provincial capital of Urumqi, further to the
west, with the rest of China. Investment in
railway services in past decades has been
enormous; a priority has been to link the
most remote regions with the big cities.

GEORG GERSTER

*P*lumes from factory smokestacks are signposts to prosperity in the big Inner Mongolian industrial center of Baotou. Fifty years ago, deer and antelope roamed the grasslands where 800 000 people now work in iron, steel, aluminum, chemical and fertilizer plants.

*O*verflow gates raised, Yangtze River waters pour furiously through the spillways of Gezhouba dam in Hubei. One of a series of dramatic engineering works destined to tame China's greatest river, the dam also provides energy for hydroelectric power.

GEORG GERSTER

A structure that rouses intense national pride, the immense bridge over the Yangtze at Nanjing is an iron shackle that binds the north and south. Originally planned with Soviet help, it seemed that the bridge was doomed when the Russian engineers and contractors walked off the job when Moscow and Beijing split in 1962. However, spurred on by Mao Zedong, Chinese workers rolled up their sleeves and carried determinedly on. When the four-mile bridge and approaches were finished in 1968 there was celebration throughout the nation. The bridge has two levels: a two-track system carries railways on the lower deck, a four-lane highway runs above.

A string of barges is pulled under one of the many bridges of Suzhou that cross the Grand Canal. Pedestrians walk above the historic waterway, which for twenty-four centuries has carried commerce between the Yangtze and the Yellow River.

DAN BUDNIK

*L*arge locks on the Yangtze take busy river traffic up in a series of steps past the dam at Gezhouba. Nearby Iching, at the mouth of the lower Yangtze Gorges, was for long a major inland port and important terminal for deep-draft vessels.

*L*ike a family of ducks paddling down a rural stream, a string of barges proceeds down the Grand Canal at Suzhou.

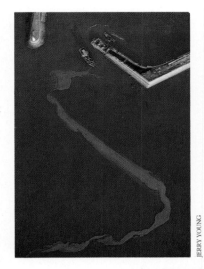

A streaky line of spilled waste from a
fishing boat writes a vivid inscription on the
waters of Shantou harbor.

JERRY YOUNG

*H*elped downstream by the current, a
flotilla of working vessels steams along the
Huangpu River.

GEORG GERSTER

*C*hugging upstream, a trio of linked barges
takes machinery parts to Shanghai factories.
Booming foreign trade has created a
demand for efficient cargo-handling
facilities. In ports all along the coast
massive new concrete wharves with
towering cranes are ready to load and
unload cargoes.

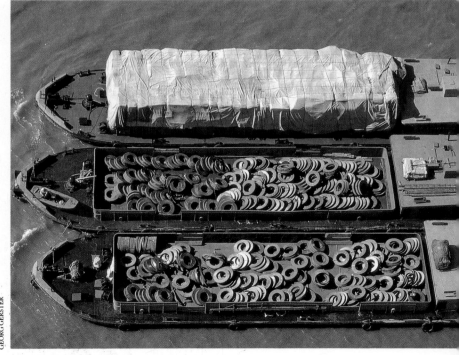

GEORG GERSTER

*L*oaded with sand for construction work, barges plod toward industrial Shanghai. The heaped loads resemble *man tou,* the delicious steamed bread buns that accompany a hearty lunch for the workers who man the wharves and factories.

GEORG GERSTER

*B*earing the names and logos of international shipping lines, stacked containers on Shanghai docks testify to China's booming export trade.

GEORG GERSTER

GEORG GERSTER

*O*ne of the greatest engineering feats of all time, the Grand Canal was hacked out of the earth in a series of works begun 2400 years ago. For more than 1700 years, successive dynasties enlarged, deepened and strengthened the walls of the artery that carried so much of China's internal trade. Many of the canals that once made the back streets of Suzhou a scenic delight have now been reclaimed, but the city still takes pride in its role as a major port on the Grand Canal. With a history stretching back at least 2500 years, Suzhou enjoyed a lengthy period when the arts blossomed, prosperous merchants subsidized painters and writers, and the visiting Marco Polo wondered at '6000 bridges carved in stone' which spanned the canals.

*W*ith so much internal trade dependent on 65 000 navigable rivers and canals, the nation stresses the construction of cargo vessels for inland waterways. This shipyard in Nanjing, where the Yangtze flows deep and wide, specializes in deep-drawing barges, riverine workhorses that will never see the open ocean.

VIEWS OF THE COUNTRY

From above, the signs of prosperity in many provinces are obvious. Television aerials take electronic sophistication from the cities to remote hamlets; modern farmhouses erected in the past decade stand beside smaller older homes. Even the crops have changed. China's farmers now supply feed grain to commercial meat-producers, and fibers and other cash crops for the textile and clothing industries. Flying over a valley in Zhejiang province, one sees fields that are vibrant with life. It is a landscape that could have come from the easel of an abstract artist: vivid scarlet, glowing shades of purple, gleaming liquid gold. These farmers are using fields not needed for their grain quota to grow flowers for the cities.

The shape of the land was changed long ago. Patient sculptors, the peasants terraced hillsides to create flat fields. If there was not enough land on the plains to grow the grain needed to support an ever-increasing population, nor to pay rent to greedy landlords and taxes to oppressive rulers, plots had to be hacked out of the hills. As the helicopter whirls through the unlikely limestone karsts of Guizhou and hovers alongside the spectacular loess landscapes of Shanxi, land made by man can be observed in all its labor-intensive diversity. Prodigious amounts of toil went into rebuilding these slopes to make 'fields-in-the-sky,' as they are known in western Sichuan. It was agonizing backbreaking work that lasted for centuries. Spectacular the sight may be; it is also humbling to contemplate the frightful physical cost of molding nature's design to the requirements of mankind.

Rural work patterns are deeply ingrained. The philosopher Han Fei, writing two centuries before the Christian era, told the parable of the peasant working in the field who saw a startled hare dash past. The animal ran into a tree and broke its neck. The farmer thought this was ideal; all he had to do was sit in his field and wait for the animals to come to him. He abandoned his hoe and patiently sat on the irrigation levee to await the next windfall. No more hares appeared. In time, the fields became unproductive, choked by weeds, and the farmer starved. The moral is simple and has a direct connection with a similar Western fable: as ye sow, so shall ye reap.

Eight out of every ten Chinese people live in the countryside. From the beginnings of the first cities, town dwellers have lived off the toil of those on the land, and the aim of every ruler since the first civilization has been to feed the vast population. Some have succeeded; most have failed. Grain production is still a sensitive issue in China, and despite the more recent emphasis on industrial expansion it is monitored carefully. China is now producing so much grain that it exports rice and other crops. For those Chinese who have lived through famine, having surplus grain is as much a sign of the success of rural reform as any number of television aerials or Western-style hotels in their cities.

*T*he Inner Mongolian terrain ranges from open
steppes to mountains to deserts and, as here, pockets of
intensively cultivated agriculture.

*A*cross the fertile Red Basin of Sichuan, so called for its soil rather than the proud revolutionary tradition, a train cuts through fields and villages on a journey to the capital of Chengdu. Railways are the steel sinews of China's economic vitality; more than 20 000 miles of tracks link the nation in a web of lines. The extensive network, much of it over inhospitable and dangerous terrain, has been built at the cost of enormous investment and effort.

*P*rovincial geographers count more than 4700 waterways in Hunan, ranging from tiny streams which water upland rice paddies to the flood of the Yangtze. Of 9.9 million acres of cultivated land, more than 80 per cent is in paddy, making Hunan one of China's major ricebowls.

140

Previous pages

*O*ases and rivers bring welcome greenery to the dun-colored escarpments of rainless Turpan in Xinjiang. The grapes grown in the Turpan Depression were noted by adventurers long before Marco Polo trudged this way along the Silk Road. At 650 feet below sea level, the Hami Depression is the lowest point in China. Turpan itself is 525 feet beneath the level of the far-distant sea.

*W*ild as the wind, horses roam the Inner Mongolian grasslands. Untamed from birth, the horses when captured, broken and trained provide ideal mounts for the nomads of the steppes.

WU SHOUZHUANG

*T*he Inner Mongolian fields etched by checkerboard patterns of crops indicate the newly won prosperity of farmers near Fengzhen. Much of this once-lonely area is now populated by Han farmers who have moved into the region as eager settlers.

Overleaf

*S*et neatly amid strip-planted fields, farming settlements dot the wide northern plains of Heilongjiang. Beneath the black earth are the country's largest oil reserves, estimated at 2500 million tons. Hardy nomadic tribes such as Ewenkis and Oroqens, linked by anthropologists to the ancestors of North American Eskimos, hunt for food in the dense forests that cover half of Heilongjiang's 178 000 square miles.

*M*odernization of agriculture has helped to change the face of the Inner Mongolian plains. Today's farmers use tractors to increase farm yields. Here, neatly aligned stacks of grain await threshing amid productive irrigated fields.

WU SHOUZHUANG

*T*he backs of houses in the Inner
Mongolian capital Hohhot are stout blank
walls facing north, giving protection from
the bitter winter winds. Southern exposure
opens the front of the houses to the
sunlight. Each home has a private
courtyard. The million people in the Inner
Mongolian capital work in industries based
on such traditional occupations as
leatherware and wool, and increasingly on
iron and steel.

*M*ongolian farmers grow wheat, oats,
millet, sorghum, maize and potatoes in the
market gardens surrounding Hohhot, as
well as cash crops such as castor oil, sugar
beet, linseed and rapeseed. The initial
processing and storage of crops takes place
in an open field on the outskirts of the
provincial capital.

Rural isolation lured Mao Zedong and the
inner cadre of his revolutionary followers to
Ruijin in 1927. At this small town in
Jiangxi the worker—peasant government
was established and from here the Red
Army broke out of the stranglehold of
enemy armies to begin the epic Long
March. Today little trace remains in the
quiet countryside of the ferocious battles
that swept over the area half a century ago
when modern China was born.

GEORG GERSTER

*J*iangsu boasts of being the richest province in the land, a region blessed by both fertile soils and abundant industry. Farmers near the old city of Suzhou take in the crops. Some fields are bare with paddystalks stacked neatly in piles, in others the harvest is under way, and patches of dark green indicate where grain is still ripening.

GEORG GERSTER

*M*eandering through farmland between
Wuxi and Suzhou, the Grand Canal is linked
with tributaries. Lifeline for a dozen
dynasties, the waterway is usually bustling
with vessels.

GEORG GERSTER

*T*he villagers of Oxhide Pond in the foothills of Anhui build a prosperous life on crops of rice and tea. New economic laws have allowed peasants to raise cash crops which have significantly boosted their personal wealth.

Following pages

*T*he high plains of Qinghai are mostly pastoral lands, but where water is available wheat and other crops are harvested. Economic planners envisage vastly expanding agricultural output in the empty high plateau steppes with growing use of modern equipment. Sheaves of wheat in the autumn sun await collection on the outskirts of the provincial capital of Xining.

Right

*E*very inch of arable flat land precious, farmers squeeze their crops up to the flanks of the steep hills of Jiangxi. With 61 7500 square miles, the province has 34 million people, of whom 85 per cent live and work on the land.

JERRY YOUNG

JERRY YOUNG

*M*ankind has long prospered on the fertile earth of Yunnan. Not far from the provincial capital of Kunming at Yuanmou archeologists have unearthed remains of a primitive human forebear who lived 1.7 million years ago. Today, a good living is still made from the rich red soil. Yunnan boasts more than 15 000 species of plants, more than any other area in China, giving rise to the provincial claim that it is a natural botanical garden. Farmers grow cash crops like rubber, shellac and quinine as well as vegetables. The countryside is marked by gently rolling hills, well drained and watered by frequent summer rains. Renowned for its Puer tea, the province also produces other teas which are admired by gourmets all over the nation.

*D*istinctive local clays produce gray tiles
for the rooftops of a village near Kunming.
The thick whitewashed walls create cool
interiors which provide a retreat from the
tropical summer heat.

JERRY YOUNG

WU SHOUZHUANG

*C*ycling or strolling home through rural lanes, farmers pass ripening and harvested fields at Yangshuo in Guangxi.

WU SHOUZHUANG

*T*hroughout China, terraces slice across the land and snake up the hillsides like giant staircases. Developed in the early years of Chinese agriculture as a means of producing areas of flat arable land in a sometimes hostile environment, terracing also helps to prevent runoff of heavy rains and is thus a valuable weapon in the battle against erosion. Here, the patterns of this rural landscaping are revealed in the brown earth of Gansu *(above)* and the green ridges of Inner Mongolia *(right)*.

IMPRESSIONS OF THE CITY

GEORGE MITCHELL

*T*aking the night air after a blistering summer day, two of Shanghai's citizens sit on a risky perch on an old mansion near the Bund.

*C*ity lights illuminate the waterfront area of Shanghai. Mostly built when the city was an international settlement ruled as a treaty port, the Bund-side structures were headquarters for the great trading houses of international mercantile concerns.

*D*uring the frenzy of the Cultural Revolution, some of the most beautiful examples of traditional architecture were destroyed. Such was the richness of culture, however, that most were spared the turbulence. In Foshan, a noted ceramics center in the lush Pearl River delta, the upswept eaves of a family temple stand proudly amid venerable banyan trees.

*O*ne of the wealthiest and most densely populated areas of China, the Pearl River delta around Guangzhou is a tropical land of fish farms, brimming paddyfields and bustling villages. It is to here that most Overseas Chinese in the Americas, Australia and Southeast Asia can trace their ancestry. In crowded village ancestral halls, geneological records are kept that permit visitors of Chinese descent to trace their family roots. Guangdong's 60 million people live in a province of 85 000 square miles that sprawls luxuriantly along the southern coast.

DAN BUDNIK

DAN BUDNIK

*T*he scenic naval base and port city of Qingdao on the southern coast of Shandong was occupied by Germans for sixteen years at the turn of the century. The area enjoys a balmy climate, produces some of China's best white wines, is home of the noted Qingdao brewery and boasts a hearty culinary tradition.

GEORG GERSTER

*U*rumqi now has skyscraper office blocks
on the site where a generation ago ragged
nomads rested their camels after treks
across the bleak deserts of Central Asia.

DAN BUDNIK

*A*t the turn of the century, Qingdao was wrested by Germany from the weak Manchu Dynasty. Although they occupied the city for a mere sixteen years, until Japan took possession on the outbreak of World War 1, the Germans left a permanent mark on Qingdao's architecture. Solid stone villas, now mostly used as tourist hotels, have brought comparisons between this great naval base and towns on the Rhine.

*M*odern beach pavilions line the shoreline at Qingdao, standing in contrast to an old Teutonic baronial hall.

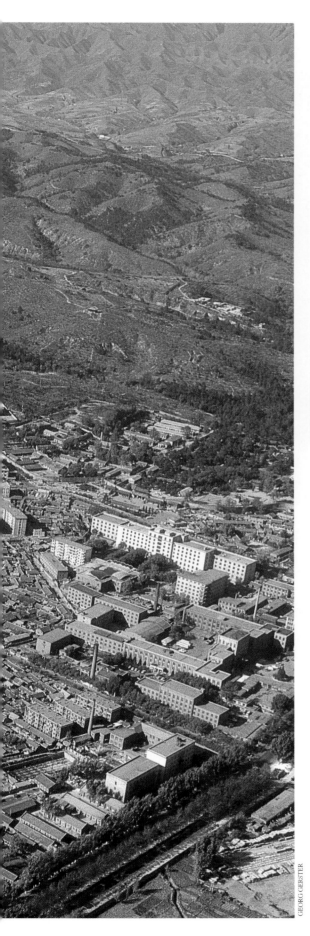

GEORG GERSTER

GEORG GERSTER

*U*nder the red flag with its five golden stars, children in a Hebei schoolyard go through morning physical exercise lessons.

*T*he city of Chengde lies within the bleak, barren and uncompromising hills of Hebei. Once an imperial resort for Qing emperors and their courts, the city today is a flourishing industrial center.

GEORG GERSTER

*I*ndustrial powerhouse in the frozen north, Jiamusi in Heilongjiang is one of a dozen manufacturing hubs that have sprung into prominence in the past decades. Once an ice-bound fishing hamlet, its deep-water port now carries sophisticated goods from aluminum smelters, farm machinery plants and plastics factories to overseas markets. Locally, the rare and exotic ginseng root is grubbed from the earth by enthusiastic ethnic Koreans who consider the long tuber to have medicinal benefits.

*B*road banyans and camphors shade a temple courtyard in Suzhou from the hot summer sun.

*C*ity of rivers and lakes, Wuxi can proudly trace a history that stretches back 3000 years. It was once an artisans' town known as Youxi ('Have Tin'), famed for its tinsmiths. Then the mines ran out, and the city changed its name to reflect its fortunes; since 25AD it has been called Wuxi ('No Tin'). The city has many other attractions, however, not least its parks, gardens and silken arts.

*N*anjing was once national capital astride the Yangtze. In 1937 it was the scene of one of the most brutal chapters in China's long and bloody history when an invading Japanese army put the city to the torch, its occupants to the sword. Skyscrapers today tower over red-tiled city roofs.

*A*s colossal as the river it crosses, the bridge over the Yangtze at Nanjing is a masterpiece of Chinese engineering and a proud example of national self-sufficiency.

WU SHOUZHUANG

*S*tanding in the path of many conquerors, the Ningxia capital of Yinchuan has been leveled many times over the centuries. Yinchuan is a pleasant town amid the vast irrigation area of the upper Huanghe. Many of the local canals are dated back to the Han Dynasty and have been in continuous use for 2000 years.

WU SHOUZHUANG

The stone houses of Chongwu huddle near the port on the Fujian coast. The province is home to wanderers, fishermen, explorers, and emigrants, and its people are proud to boast that they sailed out to explore the South Seas. Their trade goods from Song Dynasty times can be found as far afield as Borneo.

PAUL LAU

*P*erched on a rocky peak, the Potala Palace towers over Lhasa. For many centuries the palace was the home of the Dalai Lama, the spiritual leader of the Tibetan Buddhists. From the walls of this ancient palace, pilgrims and visitors can look down to the city below or up to the encircling mountains and heavens.

*P*rostrating themselves in prayer, Tibetans throw themselves energetically onto chill, ancient flagstones outside one of the many temples in their highland holy city of Lhasa. The city is a living symbol of the Buddhist faith.

JERRY YOUNG

*T*he renowned White Pagoda of
Zhouqing, long a landmark for river
boatmen, stands proudly on the bank of the
Pearl River. Typical of southern river
towns, Zhouqing's prosperity is built on
rice, fish and trade in local goods.

*T*he Flower River curls gently through
Yangzhou. The city grew into a major
inland port when the Grand Canal was cut
through it during the Tang Dynasty. At the
same time as it waxed as a commercial
center, it flourished as a home to the arts,
with poets and painters extolling the beauty
and charm of China.

GEORG GERSTER

*I*n the far northwest of China, Xinjiang encompasses the lowest spot in China. Turpan lies in a huge depression far below sea level. Railway lines now link this harsh region with provinces to the east.

*O*ases along the fabled Silk Road have a counterpart today in the irrigated settlements of Xinjiang.

VISIONS OF THE AGES

GEORG GERSTER

*M*osque-shaped roofs of tombs mark the resting place of the faithful in the Astana graves, an ancient mausoleum near the Xinjiang city of Gaochang. Archeologists have found burial places here that predate even the earliest Islamic presence. Some artefacts date back to the third century.of the Christian era when Jin Dynasty residents were buried with rich brocades, rare silks, paper hats and clothes and leather shoes. Written on the recycled paper were land deeds, trade orders and purchase documents for slaves.

*M*etropolis of the dead, graves of Han Chinese neatly line a cemetery outside Urumqi in Xinjiang province.

*T*he empire of the Western Xia Dynasty bloomed in short-lived but splendid glory in what is now Ningxia, Gansu and Shaanxi. For two centuries, the fierce Khitan tribesmen maintained rule in the area, growing to such power that Song Dynasty rulers had to pay for their submission with gifts of silk and silver. Then the Mongol tidal wave engulfed the Xia, and the empire was drowned in rivers of blood. Burial mounds once covered with glistening stones now stand as lonely mementos to the Khitan kingdom.

WU SHOUZHUANG

PAUL LAU

*S*narling a warning, a gilded temple guard dog defies evil spirits to approach the Potala Palace, most sacred of the many lamaseries and monasteries of Tibet. Originally built on a rocky outcrop in Lhasa in the seventh century, the present Potala Palace was constructed 1000 years later in the reign of the fifth Dalai Lama. A building of rare fascination containing treasures of the ages, the Potala remains central to the Buddhist faith of the Tibetan people.

*M*onks spread a sacred woven *tanka* of Buddha onto a Tibetan hillside at the monastery of Drepung on the outskirts of Lhasa. Withdrawn from its sanctuary briefly to be adored by the faithful, this religious treasure is normally hidden in the lamasery, which dates back to the fifteenth century. On view only twice in thirty years, the long-heralded appearance of the *tanka* was occasion for religious festivities, dancing, feasting and celebrations. The several hundred monks who live within the thick granite walls of Drepung include many young Tibetans who choose to follow a vocation in their ancestral faith.

*P*leasure houses and pavilions dot the hillsides and lakes of Seven Star Crags on the West River above Guangzhou.

*E*ndowed generously with lakes, rivers and reservoirs, the Pearl River delta is also the wealthiest economic enclave in all China. Money floods back to the home counties from wealthy overseas Chinese whose relatives trace their roots to this corner of Guangdong. The money enables local authorities to build scenic attractions like this star-shaped pavilion in Shunde county outside Guangzhou.

Over China

*O*nce spiritual heartland of Chinese Buddhism, Shanxi boasts some of the most famed temples in the land. Buddhism came early to the province, and temples lavishly stud the slopes of Wutaishan, one of the premier shrines in the country. Monks brought the teachings of Lord Buddha here in the seventh century after long and hazardous journeys on foot from India. A flash of vivid color amid tiled roofs and flagstoned courtyard, a monk heads for his quiet cell for meditation.

*A*n old saying goes 'There is one path and one path only to the crest of the Flowery Mountain.' Those who climb the tortuous track are rewarded with magnificent views such as this vista of the Chess Playing Pavilion that occupies one of the summits of the sacred mountain. Emperor Taizu of the Song Dynasty is said to have played chess on this pinnacle in Shaanxi province with the meditative hermit Xi Yi; the monarch wagered the mountain on the game — and lost.

WU SHOUZHUANG

*S*tanding in reverent tiers on a Ningxia hillside overlooking the Huanghe, the Hundred and Eight Pagodas are a religious relic that marks ancient Buddhist penetration into what is now an Islamic autonomous region.

*I*n about 100AD, Han Dynasty generals pressing into the wild frontier of present-day Xinjiang constructed a mighty citadel on the steep ramparts above the rivers at Jiaohe, outside Turpan. Linchpin of border defence in the Han Dynasty, this natural fortress flanked by two rivers was destroyed by the all-conquering Mongols 1200 years later. Archeologists can still trace outlines of city walls, barracks, dungeons and houses of prayer.

*T*hrough the forbidding landscape of Hebei, the Great Wall snakes over a series of mountain crests. It was to prevent the plunder of the cities on the northern plains that rulers of ducal states started building massive fortifications five centuries before the Christian era. When the mighty warlord Qin Shihuang united all China into an empire in 221BC, one of his first acts was to dispatch General Meng Tian with 300 000 men to pacify the Hun. The army worked for a decade linking together ducal walls and strengthening the structure. Millions of soldiers, skilled masons and peasants impressed as slaves toiled on successive walls. It was all to little avail: Huns, Jurchen, Mongols and Manchus pierced or swarmed over the fortification to harass China.

WU SHOUZHUANG

*S*trategic key to the gateway to China, the stronghold of the Jiayu Pass in Gansu was the fortress that guarded the narrow gap between the Qilian Range and Black Mountain in northern Gansu. Marking the western fringe of the Great Wall, the fortification controlled access to the narrow Hexi Corridor which led invaders into the Chinese heartland. Walls 33 feet high surrounded the garrison town, topped by castled pagodas which gave protection to bowmen and infantry troops ready to fight off intruders. Through immense barbican strongpoints, cavalry galloped out through iron-plated gates to do battle with barbarian raiders threatening the settled farmlands sheltered behind the wall.

*S*tarting from the Gulf of Bohai, where the Great Wall runs into the sea at Shanhaiguan, this mighty structure curves westward for 3750 miles through seven provinces and autonomous regions until it disappears into the sands at Jiayu Pass in distant Gansu. A series of ramparts, gates, strongpoints, guardhouses, beacon towers and fortresses stud the wall.

DAN BUDNIK

*C*arved with fervor for over a thousand years, the cliffs at Luoyang were once adorned with more than 100 000 images of the Buddha and his disciples. Looking out over the calm River Yi about twelve miles from the old imperial capital of Luoyang in Henan, some 97 000 of them today remain standing. Foreign curio seekers in the nineteenth century cut away many images from the cliffs and shipped them to Europe and America. Others were destroyed in religious upheavals over the centuries. But while many treasures throughout China were ruined in the upheavals of the Cultural Revolution, Luoyang was largely spared Red Guard vandalism on a mass scale. Sitting 56 feet high, the supreme deity Vairocana dominates the Fengxiansi Cave, centerpiece of the cliff-face complex.

Right

*T*he tombs of monks who died in the thousand years between Tang and Qing dynasties, a forest of pagodas bear witness to generations of learned Buddhist scholars. In the nearby Shaolin temple, the high-kicking, hard-hitting monks of the Henan hills developed the form of self-defence that was to become known as *kung fu*.

GEORG GERSTER

*R*esolving to impress warriors of his own conquering race, Emperor Kang Xi of the Qing Dynasty determined to build a city of treasure domes and pleasure palaces in the grim hills of the Manchu homeland. Work began on the enormous complex at Chengde in what is now Hebei province in 1703. It was another eighty-seven years before architects and a later emperor were satisfied that construction was complete. Bridges and connected artificial lakes were built in the style of gracious southern cities like Suzhou and Hangzhou while other parts of the park held northern buildings within glades of pine and cypress. Temples reflect Han, Tibetan and Mongolian styles as well as Manchu architecture.

WU SHOUZHUANG

WU SHOUZHUANG

*P*assing through avenues of carved courtiers, camels and imaginary beasts, millions of people every year visit the awesome burial places of the rulers of the Ming Dynasty. Deep underground, rock-lined caverns were prepared to hold the bodies of the departed rulers; the remains of some of the thirteen emperors buried in the valley of Shisanling have still to be excavated. The last resting place of Emperor Yong Le took eighteen years to build; when he was buried, sixteen living concubines were entombed with his corpse. Half a million workers were whipped and bribed to build the necropolis of Wan Li, who celebrated the completion of the works by throwing a party in the huge cavern. One of the most popular tourist sites in China, the Ming tombs are well-preserved monuments. Future archeological digs may reveal many more relics.

In flight over Yangshuo near Guilin are joint publisher Zhou Wanping and Hong Kong Balloon Club president Mike Bradley.

A FLIGHT OF FANTASY

Whenever we talked about our plan, we kept hearing the same response. '*Tai fuza!*' 'Too difficult! Too complicated!' Perhaps our ambitious proposal seemed too fantastic: we wanted to produce the first aerial photographic book to cover the whole of China.

The problem was not one of cost, or logistics, or lack of suitable photographers, but of permission. 'You must have the permission of the appropriate authorities,' we were told. 'Who are the appropriate authorities?' we asked. 'The security of the airways of China is the responsibility of the People's Liberation Army; they will never give you permission to fly over China.'

'We can but ask,' we thought. We had just completed an international joint-venture book project with the China National Publishing Industry Trading Corporation to commemorate and celebrate the fiftieth anniversary of the Long March, and we knew that several of the Army's leaders of today had served in that momentous and historic campaign. At a dinner to launch our book in Beijing's Great Hall of the People, we cautiously raised the project again with a veteran of the Long March, who was now a senior member of the Central Military Commission.

'The project,' we were told, 'is extremely worthwhile. The Army will be most supportive. There is much outstanding subject matter to be photographed from above China. It will be another act of cooperation between the Chinese people and yourselves.'

Not only would the People's Liberation Army give us the necessary permission to photograph every province of the mainland from the air, but also the Army would provide

An early-morning ascent over the distinctive hills of Guilin.

Pre-flight checks in Guilin with balloon pilot Paul Gianniotis (left) and *Over China* photographers Wu Shouzhuang and Dan Budnik.

JERRY YOUNG

aircraft from which to photograph. In addition, the Army would lend us its finest, most experienced aerial photographer to fly with our foreign photographers. And, since the Army had its own photographic publishing division, the Great Wall Publishing House, why did we not form a joint venture with them?

We left China in a high state of excitement. Not only had we secured the necessary permission, but also we had the resources of the world's largest military organization to help us achieve our objective. It seemed that the most difficult problem had been overcome.

Over the next six months, during the winter of 1986–87, we had little day-to-day communication with our new partners, but we were confident that the military minds in Beijing were establishing the logistical framework for our joint venture. We and our Chinese partners each produced a list of a hundred suggested photographic subjects. There was a 70 per cent

While we waited for Georg Gerster to fly in from Zurich to start what was to be for him a four-month odyssey, we spoke with British Army medical specialists on the necessary vaccinations and inoculations to keep our photographers fit in China (typhoid, tetanus, polio, Japanese encephalitis, hepatitis 'A' and malaria) and assembled 'comfort kits' for them to take with them — instant coffee, teabags, milk powder, toothpaste, aspirin, pills for diarrhoea and constipation, sun cream, mosquito repellant. Our caution proved ungrounded, since the photographers were well cosseted by their PLA hosts.

Georg Gerster's first sortie into southeast China proved an unpropitious start to the project. The one factor neither partner could plan for, bad weather, set in with a vengeance. Summer monsoons spread clouds and haze in an unpenetrable miasma across the land. In an uncomfortable honeymoon the new joint-venture partners endeavored to make the best of a bad job, but eventually, as long-range weather forecasts promised more of the same, the scheduled shoot was postponed until better weather prevailed. Georg returned to Zurich.

In early August Georg Gerster returned to Beijing to begin photography in the west. It had been resolved that Georg would fly with the PLA's experienced photographer Wu Shouzhuang to film the erosion-torn lands of Shaanxi, the windswept grasslands of Inner Mongolia, the Gobi Desert and the far western province of Xinjiang, on the borders of the Soviet Union. To Georg, Xinjiang was one of the main reasons he had taken on the assignment: he would be the first Western photographer to film this

In Heilongjiang, Georg Gerster (center) with M1-8 helicopter crew and project coordinator Li Qianguang (on Gerster's right).

remote and fascinating region from the air. For Wu Shouzhuang, there was a different excitement. With characteristic modesty he recalled:

'I was to accompany Mr Gerster in an M1-8 helicopter flying from Beijing to Inner Mongolia. This was to be the beginning of our joint cooperation, and I felt honored as he is a world-famous photographer and there would be many opportunities for me to learn from him.'

After Xinjiang, Gerster and Wu split up, Gerster to go to the northeast and the wheatlands and forests of Heilongjiang, and Wu to photograph the western extremities of the Great Wall in Ningxia, the sweeping Yellow River and the salt lakes of Qinghai. On his return to Hong Kong, Georg commented: 'In twenty years of aerial photography all over the world I have never photographed such diversity of images within a single assignment.'

Meanwhile Paul Lau had been using his fluency in Putonghua, the national language of China, to gain access to a variety of natural and man-made high points, ranging from city skyscrapers to the slopes of the sacred

Refueling the sturdy AN-2 near Yuzhong in Lanzhou. These multipurpose biplanes were the only fixed-wing aircraft used during the project.

mountains. Working independently, he covered locations from Beijing to Lhasa, taking high-angle photographs of everything from street markets to mountain ranges.

In Beijing and Hong Kong we were making the final arrangements for the ten-day hot-air balloon expedition in Guilin (see inset feature). The ballooning provided an opportunity for Mr Wu to work with the other two foreign aerial photographers, Jerry Young and Dan Budnik, who were to start their assignments in Guilin before separating to go to different provinces.

For Dan Budnik the most memorable moment of his China

JERRY YOUNG

On a tethered balloon flight in Guilin, youngsters lift off with balloon pilot Adam Takach.

Dan was to experience the aerial photographer's greatest concern, bad weather. He recounted the story: 'Weather complications set in whilst attempting the photograph the Yangtze River gorges, and a scheduled one-day shoot stretched into a week. Each day the weather became worse, more rain and darkness, zero visibility. Unable to fly, I found the tedium was alleviated only by a daily walk down the hill into the town of Dangyang, where I became a foreign curiosity, to be followed shamelessly. On what was to be my last walk into the town, two schoolgirls followed me for blocks, disappeared, then hastily confronted me with a written note. My interpreter translated; it was a note of welcome on behalf of their entire school to their foreign friend. Suddenly, even dismal Dangyang was transformed into a most precious place.

To Budnik, on his first visit to China, the most lasting image was the 'endless undulating sea of terraced hills and mountains, lovingly and painfully cultivated to help feed China's millions. It was then I could see the effects of this enormous population at work, a work that took on artistic greatness.'

Jerry Young, photographing in southern China in October, was much more fortunate with his weather. With many hours of experience of flying in military aircraft, Young was particularly impressed by his pilots. 'It is unusual to find such good aircrew anywhere. I was intrigued to note that all the pilots looked like the classic image of a pilot even though they were Chinese. They were true "Battle of Britain hero" types — strong line to the jaw, swaggering, tough but good-hearted. The image transcends national boundaries.'

schedule was a balloon flight over Guilin with Mr Wu. 'Foul overcast weather dramatically gave way to clear blue sky just in time for our launch in spectacular late-afternoon light. It was my first hot-air balloon flight, one of intense beauty, with the greenery of cultivated fields contrasting with those ubiquitous grey-green peaks. This flight was doubly exciting as we crash-landed in a farmer's field. I will never forget Mr Wu's inscrutable expression slipping slightly between the first and second bounces of that landing.'

After his ballooning Dan went north to photograph the coastal province of Shandong and then followed the Yangtze River upstream.

reminisced: 'On my last day the director and deputy director of the Great Wall Publishing House, Mr Li Tingsong and Mr Zhou Wanping, took me for a farewell lunch at the famous Peking Duck restaurant, then dropped me off at the Forbidden City. I'm not ashamed to say that I was close to tears to think I wouldn't see them again.'

Wu Shouzhuang, photographing his own country, was more pragmatic. 'After finishing the shooting of our final location, we took a deep breath, releasing the tension of the last two months. I felt like a coolie relaxing after a long journey, laying off his burden.'

All the 85 000 photographs taken in China were couriered to Australia for processing, and during November 1987 edited down to 2000 images. In December the Chinese partners met with us in Hong Kong to review the photographs selected. In Sydney the editorial team and the designer conferred day after day, trying to choose just 250–300 photographs that would do justice to the extraordinary scenery of the world's most populous country. *Over China*, once a flight of fantasy, had become a reality.

Publisher John Owen indicates a flight path to interpreter Wang Lei (left) as joint publisher Zhou Wanping and Balloon Club president Mike Bradley look on.

Ballooning in Guilin

Elderly citizens of Guilin, practising their early morning ritual of 'shadow boxing' exercises in Seven Star Park, had never seen anything like it. As the first glimmer of dawn pierced the mist-clad crags surrounding this picturesque spot in southern Guangxi province, two slumbering giants stretched out on the ground slowly came to life. With a dragon's fiery breath, high-pressure gas burners roared, pumping 150 000 cubic feet of heated air into the vast multicolored envelopes of two hot-air balloons. As onlookers watched in amazement, green-uniformed soldiers from the People's Liberation Army and Westerners clad in white overalls scurried about with guide ropes in a weirdly choreographed Maypole dance coaxing the massive 80-foot-high balloons into the lightening sky.

Hot-air balloons were reputedly invented in China in the twelfth century AD when they were used in battle by the Mongols for signaling and as regimental standards, but it was not until the mid-1980s when balloons carrying people were seen in the skies of China. Hot-air balloons, however, provide a near-perfect platform for aerial photography, and to the organizers of *Over China* the opportunity of using balloons seemed too good to overlook.

The area selected for this unusual and exciting photographic safari was the unique limestone karst country of Guilin, in the northeastern part of Guangxi province, about 300 miles northeast of Hong Kong. The image that most Westerners have of the landscape of China is in fact the

Between the limestone peaks of Guilin the plain is intensively farmed.

landscape of Guilin, where steep craggy hills spring suddenly from a lush green plain and stretch in blue-grey battlements into the hazy distance. This curiously formed range of limestone peaks, thrust up from the seabed 300 million years ago and eroded over millennia by wind and water, has been the inspiration of Chinese painters and poets for centuries. The Tang Dynasty poet Han Yu (768–824) captured the region's beauty in his celebrated lines:

*'The river is a blue silk ribbon,
and the hills, like blue jade hairpins.*

The ten-day balloon expedition was organized like a military expedition, with detailed planning over five months. Whilst the publishing division of the Chinese People's Liberation Army in Beijing liaised with units of the PLA Political and Logistics Departments in Guangzhou, and with the Armed Police Force and Air Traffic Control in Guilin, a growing task force in Hong Kong began coordinating and assembling more than 5 tons of equipment, fuel and '*matériel.*'

At Xingping, balloons are tethered by the Li River as the sun sets behind the karst peaks.

It was fortunate that one of the world's most experienced balloon clubs was based in Hong Kong. Organizers approached the Hong Kong Balloon and Airship Club, which, although of amateur status, has several commercial airline pilots and aircrew among its active membership who hold a number of world hot-air balloon records. The club had never flown its balloons in the mainland of China, and members were enthusiastic to participate in what promised to be a unique and memorable expedition. However, their experience in flying in out-of-the-way places around the world forewarned

them of several problems that needed to be overcome.

One immediate apparent problem was that of fuel. Hot-air balloons may fly on hot air, but correctly formulated and calibrated liquid gas is required not only to inflate the balloon's envelope, but also to keep it 'topped up' with hot air as it flies over the countryside. The ideal gas for ballooning is a mixture of 80 per cent propane, 20 per cent butane, but this is unobtainable in China, where the locally available liquid petroleum gas is suitable for cooking but does not develop enough calorific heat for hot-air ballooning. Companies

of the Royal Dutch Shell Group in Hong Kong and Shenzhen in China came to the expedition's rescue by providing 6000 liters of a specially formulated gas mixture from their Chinese joint-venture fuel depot in Shekou, near the Hong Kong border.

Another problem emerged through a sponsor's generosity. Six weeks before scheduled lift-off in Guilin, DHL Worldwide Express agreed to provide a new 77 000 cubic foot balloon for the expedition and for later donation to the balloon club. This particular model of balloon, because of its size, carrying capacity and manoeuvreability, was to

THE SPONSORS

Over China could not have been produced without the support of its sponsors. A project of this magnitude, involving the coordination of the skills of so many people and the use of so much complex equipment and technology, depends on the help, goodwill and active sponsorship of many companies. To those listed below we offer our heartfelt thanks.

Bond Corporation Holdings Limited of Australia, whose core businesses are brewing, media and communications, property, and energy resources, has been active in China for many years and is continuing to seek out new business opportunities there. Bond Corporation holds a 30 per cent interest in the oil exploration joint venture on Hainan Island, off southern China. In 1986 a new subsidiary, Bond Corporation International Limited, was established in Hong Kong to act as the principal holding company for Bond's operations outside Australia. The Bond Group chose Hong Kong as its international base because it is one of the financial centers of the world's most populous region, is at the heart of the Southeast Asian business region and has a pivotal role to play in the future development of China.

Cathay Pacific Airways is the airline of Hong Kong. Founded in Hong Kong in 1946 Cathay Pacific was initially a regional airline serving the major Asian cities. In the mid 1970s the airline started operations to Bahrain and shortly afterwards to London employing its long-range Boeing 747. More recent new destinations include Vancouver, San Francisco, Rome, Paris, Bali, Nagoya, Kaohsiung, Amsterdam and Zurich. Cathay Pacific has achieved a unique reputation for assisting its passengers to 'arrive in better shape' through the care and attention of a professional staff and through the highest standards of technical competence. Cathay Pacific serves Shanghai and Beijing from its Hong Kong base.

DHL International is the world's largest international air express company with over 800 offices in more than 175 countries. DHL's global network was further strengthened with the signing of an exclusive joint-venture agreement with Sinotrans, the China National Foreign Trade Transportation Corporation. This resulted in expanding Sinotrans' operations worldwide through the extensive DHL network and, in turn, opened up the growing market in China to DHL International and its clients. DHL provides service to and from China out of three gateway cities: Beijing, Guangzhou and Shanghai.

HILL AND KNOWLTON

Hill and Knowlton was the first international public relations agency to open an office in Beijing, in 1984, and remains the only full-service international agency on site in China. The firm's China Division, with offices in Beijing and Hong Kong, has close working relationships with China's media and with key government and commercial organizations in Beijing and in important regional markets such as Shanghai and Guangzhou. The China Division enables multinational corporations to conduct comprehensive communications programs in one of the world's most challenging markets. The Division also provides public relations counsel to Chinese organizations doing business overseas. The China Division is backed by Hill and Knowlton's global network of offices providing media, corporate, financial and government relations counsel and full support services.

Hutchison Whampoa Limited

Hutchison Whampoa Limited, which has had links with China for more than a century, is one of Hong Kong's largest and most successful investment holding and trading companies. With highly diversified business interests in property, container terminal operations, power generation, trading, retailing, quarrying, telecommunications, and oil and gas, the HWL Group of companies is well positioned and committed to furthering trade relations with China.

The ICI Group has had trading links with China since 1898. In 1984 ICI (China) opened a liaison office in Beijing to handle the development of the Group's growing China business. ICI has the widest range of products of any chemicals manufacturer and is actively promoting those most suited to China's modernization program. These products include agrochemicals, industrial and specialty chemicals, dyestuffs and pigments, paints and coatings. ICI's growing commitment to China includes the sponsorship of study visits by Chinese students to the United Kingdom.

Companies of the Royal Dutch Shell Group have been active in China Shenzhen and Hong Kong for many decades. During the 1980s particular emphasis has been given by Shell to the development of business in the People's Republic of China. In 1981 Shell China was established with an office in Beijing, and at about the same time Shell companies based in Hong Kong increased their oil and chemicals marketing efforts, mainly in Guangdong province and the Shenzhen SEZ. Shell's activities in China now include oil exploration, marketing of oil and chemical products, coal minerals, timber, and the processing of Chinese crude oil. Shell has built up a close working relationship with many Chinese organizations. In particular, two oil-marketing joint ventures are now in operation in Shekou (Shenzhen SEZ) along with joint-venture participation in petrol stations, packed LPG distribution and other facilities.

The Sheraton Asia Pacific Corporation's involvement in China began in earnest on 18 March 1985 when a management and marketing agreement was signed with the owners of the Great Wall Hotel in Beijing. In the few years since then, the Sheraton 'S' has become synonymous with quality accommodation in China, which meets international standards. Late in 1986 Sheraton established a presence in Shanghai with the Hua Ting Sheraton; a year later the Sheraton Tianjin was opened. Contracts have been signed for further Sheraton properties in Xi'an, Guilin and Shanghaiguan. One of the corporation's goals is to be widely represented in China's secondary cities, and a 'Sheraton Inns' concept has been especially developed to this end. Sheraton is proud to be contributing to the development of China's tourist industry while providing business travelers with efficient and caring service and catering for the growing number of international conferences being held in Chinese cities.

INDEX

agriculture, 133–5
Astana graves, 238

Baotou, 119
barges, 125, 126–7, 129
Beijing, 113, 122, 180, 181, 230–1, 237, 265, 267
   see also Summer Palace; White Dagoba
bicycles, 122, 161
boats, 90–1
   see also barges; junks
Bohai Sea, 19, 268
Boxer Rebellion, 265
brickworks, 113, 114
building industry, 112–13

Canton *see* Guangzhou
Chengde, 207, 260, 263
Chengdu, 104
Chess Playing Pavilion, 2–3, 249
children, 123, 207
China's Sorrow *see* Huanghe River
Chongwu, 218–19
coal, 88–9, 114
Crystal Palace of the Dragon King, Guilin Mountains, 164–5
Cultural Revolution, 189, 231, 237, 258

Daguang Park, Kunming, 18
Dalai Lama, 222
desert encroachment, 36, 38–9, 42
Drepung monastery, Lhasa, 244
duck farming, 105

erosion, 6, 36, 40–1, 54, 66, 162, 175
   see also desert encroachment
Ewenki people, 144–5

Fengxiansi Cave, 258
fish farming, 72, 74–7, 94–5, 98–9, 156, 168–9, 189
Flaming Mountains of Xinjiang, 34, 35, 46–7, 64–5
Flower River, 225
Flowery Mountain, Shaanxi province, 2–3, 21, 249
Foshan, 189
free enterprise *see* private enterprise

Gansu, 54, 56, 66, 73, 79, 162, 198
   agriculture, 80
Gezhouba Dam, Yangtze River, 118, 124
ginseng, 210
Gobi Desert, 36–7
Grand Canal, 9, 27, 98–9, 121, 125, 128, 151, 157, 225, 229
Great Buddha, Leshan, 250–1
Great Wall, 19, 78, 237, 255–6, 257
Green Wall, 36
Guangdong
   agriculture, 169
Guangxi Zhuang Autonomous Region, 130–1, 132

Guangzhou, 93, 183, 189, 247
Guilin, 68–9, 190–1
Guilin mountains, 4–5, 22–3, 164–5, 166–7
   see also Crystal Palace of the Dragon King; Paint Brush Peak
Han River, 84–5
harvesting, 102, 103, 110, 132, 150, 161
Hebei, 60, 207
   agriculture, 110–11
Heilongjiang, 106, 114
   agriculture, 80–1, 108–9, 144–5
Hexi Corridor, 257
Hohhot, 146, 196, 197
horse racing, 197
horses, 140–1
Huanghe River, 19, 20, 27, 38–9, 43, 78, 79, 94, 121
Huangpu River, 126, 183
Huashan Mountains, 21, 59, 242
   see also Peak of the Morning Sun
Hubei, 171
Hunan, 137
Hundred and Eight Pagodas, 252

Iching, 124
industry, 87–9, 114, 119
Inner Mongolia, 119, 140–1, 163
   agriculture, 134, 142, 143, 147
irrigation, 58, 60–1, 169, 170, 217
   karez-style, 172–3
Iron Pagoda, Kaifeng, 243

Jiamusi, 210
Jiangsu, 156
   agriculture, 150
Jiangxi, 100–1
   agriculture, 153
Jiaohe fortress, Turpan, 253
Jiayu Pass, 257
Jilin, 88
junks, 84–5, 92

Kaifeng, 243
   see also Iron Pagoda, Kaifeng
Khitan people, 240–1
kung fu, 259
Kunming, 82, 96–7, 103, 123, 160, 174, 192–3
   see also Daguang Park, Kunming

Lake Dianchi, 96–7, 103
   fish farming, 95
Lake of Heaven, Xinjiang, 53
Lake Tai, 72, 98–9
Lanzhou, 198
   railway from Xining, 67
Laojun (god), 21
Lhasa, Tibet 222
   see also Potala Palace
Li River, 4–5, 68–9, 98
Liaoning
   agriculture, 44–5
loess soil, 27, 43, 54, 79, 133–5, 175
   erosion, 6, 25
Long March, 148–9, 209

Luoyang, 258

Mao Zedong, 120, 148, 180, 209, 231, 237
   tomb, 237
market gardening, 81–2
   see also private enterprise
Ming tombs, 235, 270–1
Miyun River dam, 60–1
Mongolia, 36, 40–1, 42
   see also Inner Mongolia
motor vehicles, 89
Mudan River, 114
Mysterious Manifestation Temple, Beijing, 266

Nanchang, 100–1
Nanjing, 112, 129, 183, 214
   Treaty of, 186
Naxi people, 205–6
Ningxia, 115
Ningxia Autonomous Region, 42, 78
North China Plain, 19, 27

Oroqen people, 144–5
Oxhide Pond, 152

pagodas, 235, 252
   see also Hundred and Eight Pagodas; Iron Pagoda, Kaifeng; White Pagoda of Zhouqing
Paint Brush Peak, Guilin mountains, 164–5
paper production, 106
Peak of the Morning Sun, Huashan mountains, 59
Pearl River, 27, 74–7, 93, 189, 224–7
Penglai
   artificial harbor, 268
   redoubt, 269
petrochemicals, 115, 198
petroleum, 144–5
port facilities, 126–7
Potala Palace, Lhasa, 222, 245
poultry, 105
   see also duck farming
private enterprise, 81–2, 87–9, 152, 186
Putao, 235

Qiling ranges, 52
Qingdao, 195, 202, 203
Qinghai, 66, 67, 154–5
   see also Tibet–Qinghai Plateau
quarrying, 112

railways, 67, 116–17, 136, 192, 227
reafforestation, 54, 66
rice fields, 10–11, 62–3, 137, 164–5, 170, 189
Ruijin, 148–9, 208

salt, 107
Sanyi people, 32–3
Second Opium War, 186, 264
Seven Star Crags, 246
Shandong, 102–3
Shanghai, 81–2, 86, 126–7, 178–9, 181, 182, 184, 185, 186, 187
Shantou, 84–5, 90–1, 92, 126, 168–9, 220–1, 232–3
Shanxi, 248

Shenzhou, 110–11
Sichuan, 77, 104, 105, 112, 136, 250
Silk Road, 34, 48–9, 138–9, 226
Stone Forest of Yunnan, 32–3
street sellers, 104
Summer Palace, Beijing, 264
Suzhou, 125, 128, 150, 213, 228

Taishan mountain, 20, 235, 236
tea, 158, 159
Temple of Confucius, 234
Tengger Desert, 38–9, 42
terraces, 56–7, 162, 170, 171
terracotta warriors, Xi'an, 235
Tibet, 28, 50–1, 222
    see also Dalai Lama; Drepung monastery, Lhasa;
        Potola Palace
Tibet–Qinghai Plateau, 20, 27, 28
timber, 36, 54, 66, 106, 108–9, 144–5, 208
    see also reafforestation
transport, 67, 86, 116, 122
    see also bicycles; motor vehicles, railways
Turpan, 48–9, 116, 138–9, 227
    see also Jiaohe fortress
Turpan Depression, 25, 64–5, 138–9
    see also Flaming Mountains of Xinjiang

Urumqi, 53, 116, 199, 200, 201, 239
Uygur people, 199

Vairocana deity, 258

White Dagoba, Beijing, 266
White Pagoda of Zhouqing, 224
Wutaishan, 248
Wuxi, 213, 229

Xiamen, 204
Xin Chao people, 90–1
Xining, 154–5
    railway to Lanzhou, 67
Xinjiang, 48, 49, 53, 58, 65, 107, 172–3, 226–7
    see also Flaming Mountains of Xinjiang; Lake of
        Heaven

Yangshuo, 161
Yangtze River, 20, 27, 118, 121, 124, 129, 156
    bridge at Nanjing, 120, 214–15
    see also Gezhouba Dam
Yangzhou, 225
Yellow Mountain, 30
Yellow River see Huanghe River
Yi River, 258
Yinchuan, 216
Yuanmou,
    primitive man, 159
Yudu, 209
Yunnan, 70–1, 77, 158–9, 176–7
    agriculture, 71, 103
    see also Kunming; Stone Forest of Yunnan

Acknowledgments

Many individuals have contributed to the complex task of preparing this book. The publishers would particularly like to thank the following people:

Mandie Appleyard • Judy Arundel • Martha Avery • Nick Bailey • Wilson Banks • Kasyan Bartlett • Magnus Bartlett • Nick Beecroft • David Bell • Suzette Betteridge • Bian Chunguang • Dawn Bradley • Patrick Briggs • Woodfin Camp • Chang Zhenguo • Claire Chao • Chen Zhiren • Ben Chapman • Anna Chilvers • Kim Chui • Po Chung • Mark Collins • Peter Cook • Ron Cromie • Jan Davis • Dong Chensheng • Sue Earle • Mary-Dawn Earley • Louis Eaton • Alan Farrelly • Feng Yanmei • Anne Forrest • Anne Francis • Ian Fraser • Bubbles Frez • Gao Yanxiang • Wilbur Garrett • Gong Huaguang • Peter Greenberg • Paul Griffiths • Barry Grindrod • Gu Yulong • Guo Guiji • Guo Tianhai • Barbara Harman • Kent Harrison • Richard Hartman • Karena Hatfield • Phillip Hawkes • Brian Heap • Susan Heinz • Sheridan Hillis • Christopher Holmes • Stephanie Holmes • Hou Zhaoqiang • Huang Hongjian • Huang Jingzheng • Huang Zhihua • Tony Hudson • Alan Jennings • Jiang Mengzhen • Richard Johnson • Meinir Jones • Kate Kelly • John Kerr • Victor Kimura • Robert Kirschenbaum • Miguel Ko • Kong Lingduo • Joel de Lacey • John Leader • M.V. Lee • Li Fangtian • Li Jianhui • Li Jicheng • Li Lisheng • Li Qi • Li Tie • Li Youcheng • Li Zhidao • Tony van der Linden • Liu Datang • Liu Lianshan • Liu Zhibin • Long Wenshan • Long Yunhe • Dawn Low • Lu Jiangwen • Peter Lucas • Ma Shuxue • Ma Zhongyuan • Vincent Mang • Michelle Mannion • John Merson • William R. Moore • Charlene Murphy • Simon Murray • Brian Nairn • Chris Oliver • Roy Olsson • Jake Olver • Jennie Phillips • Ronnie Poon • Bill Porter • Nick Purvis • Qiao Yan • Qin Xinghan • Zhao Qing • Qui Xuexin • Bill Roberts • Lew Roberts • Simon Rodwell • Tom Sage • Pam Seaborn • Shen Rengan • Shi Wenbiao • Kit Sinclair • Aubrey Singer • Mary Smith • Thomas R. Smith • Jack Spackman • John Stevenson • Tan Yadong • Sue Tickner • S.H. Tu • Jirayu Vajrabhaya • Wang Fayao • Wang Hairu • Joy Wang • Wang Minghui • Wang Xiao • Wang Yongding • Richard Warburton • Glynis Watts • Wei Hui • Harold Weldon • Wen Wanan • Max Wilhelm • John Wong • Stephen Wong • Wu Jie • Wu Jun • Xu Liyi • Xu Ye • Ya Youneng • Yan Linke • Yang Shaoming • Yang Yunfang • Yu Qinglin • Yu Xiao • Yuan Qi • Zhang Huan • Zhang Qijin • Zhao Qing • Zhao Xiaopeng • Zhao Zhungwang • Zheng Qi • Yan Zhenghao • Zhong Ming • Zhou Yan • Hannes Ziegler.

The publishers would also like to thank the following Authorities in the People's Republic of China for their cooperation and help in the preparation of *Over China*:

Chinese People's Liberation Army Headquarters of the General Staff • PLA General Political Department • PLA General Logistics Department • Press and Publication Administration of the People's Republic of China • Customs General of the People's Republic of China • PLA Pictorial • PLA Photo Studio • Modern Press • PLA Air Force and air forces from various regions • PLA Navy Command and Political Department • Command and Political Department of PLA Beijing Region • Command, Political Department and Logistic Department of PLA Guangzhou Region • Command and Political Department of PLA Jinan Region • Command and Political Department of PLA Nanjing Region • Command and Political Department of PLA Chengdu Region • Command and Political Department of PLA Lanzhou Region • Command and Political Department of PLA Shenyang Region • Interpreters' Office of PLA Air Force • PLA Units of Guangzhou Region in Guilin Area • Armed Police Forces in Shenzhen and Guilin Areas • People's Revolutionary and Military Museum of China • China Central Television • Municipality of Guilin City, Guangxi • Country Government of Yangshuo, Guangxi